SAY "YES" TO LIFE

Daily Meditations
For Recovery

Father Leo Booth

Health Communications, Inc.
Deerfield Beach, FL 33442

Father Leo Booth
Emmaus Ltd.
Long Beach, California

ISBN 0-932194-46-X

Published by: Health Communications, Inc.
            Enterprise Center
            3201 S.W. 15th Street
            Deerfield Beach, FL 33442

This book is dedicated to
all those who are recovering from life.

INTRODUCTION

When I was asked to write this book I was concerned that it should be inclusive, not representing any one religion or denomination and open to every human being who was concerned with discovering their "given" spirituality on a daily basis. I also wanted to represent the compulsive and obsessive behavioral "lifestyles" that cause pain and distress in a person's life, e.g., eating disorders, gambling, adult children issues, and people who love others too much! At times it felt as if I was wearing more than one hat but I was surprised at the comfort of the fit.

These meditations are personal and I do not apologize for the use of the personal pronoun "I". They recount my struggle with a variety of topics and because human beings are so similar, I have little doubt that you will be able (regardless of background) to identify with the feelings and struggles expressed.

Talking about God is always difficult and reference to the "gender" of God has become a serious issue among many concerned Christians, particularly the feminist groups that have (quite correctly) felt ignored, abused and discounted. Sufficient to say that I believe God to be sexless, religionless and "beyond" any culture, class or creed — however, simply from the point of view of consistent style, I refer to Her as Him!!

Talking about God from the human standpoint always reflects our smallness and imperfection, and yet the fact that we can talk about Him at all reveals our inherent "greatness".

This book is not intended to convert anybody from their personal beliefs or convictions but show on a daily basis the connection between our daily lives as recovering people (whatever the addiction) with the God-given dynamic of spirituality. How we struggle with what it is to be a human being. How we fight, cry, surrender and succeed all in a single day. And how God is involved.

For the recovering "compulsive person" God is too important to miss — may you find Him now. This book is dedicated to all those who are recovering from life.

*The one serious
conviction
that a man should
have is that
nothing
is to be taken
seriously.*

Nicholas Murray Butler

"It is not that I think or believe [in spirituality]
but that I know."
Sir Arthur Conan Doyle

Some things I seem to know intuitively: and I know that spirituality is involved in and affects everything. In a human being it combines the physical, mental and emotional but it also reaches beyond the human being and connects the peoples of the world. Spirituality is the force for good and wholeness in this universe.

This is not just an opinion or a thought. It is a feeling that runs so deep in my being that I know it must be true. When I read, hear music or see movies, this feeling is often evoked, and I know God is alive in His world and wanting it to be ONE.

In the silence of Your world I know You.

*"A thing is not necessarily true because a man
dies for it."*

Oscar Wilde

I came to the conclusion in my battle with alcoholism that my involvement with God's will for me was crucial; my choice is the result of God's bestowed gift of freedom. And freedom is awfully real! The price of freedom is Auschwitz; the price of freedom is the world's starving millions; the price of freedom is the dead drunk in a derelict building. Men do insane and destructive things, usually because they think they know best. Men die to protect their ego. The sin of Adam, wanting to be like God, haunts us all.

Today I am learning to detach spiritually in order to discover a pure and selfless love. I stand back and consider before I act; often after a time of reflection I see the event differently — and it is okay to change my mind.

*Lord, I understand choice to be the key
to my humanity.*

"No man is an island, entire of itself; every man is a piece of the continent, a part of the main."
                                        John Donne

For years I thought that I was alone; lost isolated and afraid. Today I understand this to be a symptom of my alcoholism, an aspect of my disease. Alcoholism is "cunning, baffling and powerful"; it is a mystery that we have only begun to understand. One thing we know, the disease, the "ism" of alcoholism, involves more than the act of drinking. Feelings of inadequacy, isolation and fear keep us from recovering until we discover the spiritual strength to confront the disease in our lives. The initial risk of "letting go" and trusting others is an essential part of the recovery process.

When we discover that we are not alone, then relationships and hope are reactivated; life is worth living again.

O Lord, I believe I am part of this world and an important part of You.

"A hungry man is not a free man."
Adlai Stevenson

For years I craved food. It was my escape
from reality. It stopped the pain, loneliness and
anger — for a moment. It felt good. Eventually
I began to feel bad — but I could not stop.
I was addicted to sugar and sodium. My
freedom was being exchanged for doughnuts!

I heard a man talk about his compulsion
around cocaine and gambling. I asked how he
managed to abstain and he replied: "Talk about
it, a day at a time!"

Today I am compulsive about getting well,
and I talk about my disease every day. The price
of freedom is vulnerability. God is in the risk.
I have taken it.

God, let me experience freedom in the choices I
make today.

*"It's the most unhappy people who most fear
change."*
                                        Mignon McLaughlin

When I was drinking, I hated change. I hated things not being the same. I feared anything being different. Rarely did I want to go anywhere new. My attitudes were fixed and rigid. I resented any criticism of my behavior. The unexpected was seen as sabotage or a threat. My paranoia was extreme.

Today I have decided to let go of the control, the pretense and the arrogance. I face life as it comes — and today I do not drink. I am responsible for my life but I cannot control the world. Today I am learning to relax in the acceptance of my disease.

*May I always discover the courage to change the
things I can.*

"Nothing is interesting if you are not interested."
                             Helen MacInnes

There is a subtle distinction between the "dry" alcoholic and the "sober" alcoholic. The sober alcoholic chooses not to drink because he has accepted his alcoholism. The "dry" alcoholic is "not drinking" but is invariably angry and resentful — and he is not expressing these feelings. His abstinence is not exciting because he is not interested in it — he is bored.

The "dry" alcoholic is also boring to be around. Why? Because he is bored. His boredom makes him boring. He really wants to drink. He has stopped drinking for reasons that do not include the acceptance of the disease; he is still a victim of the disease.

Sobriety, by contrast, is an adventure into self. It greets the new day with enthusiasm and energy. Sobriety is the spiritual discovery of God in our lives.

Let me always remember that my interests in life reflect my interest in You.

*"I could not say I believe. I know! I have had the
experience of being gripped by something that is
stronger than myself, something that people
call God."*

                                                    Carl Jung

God is beyond our comprehension, and in
a sense we are all agnostics — none of us
KNOW know; uncertainty is part of faith.

However, there are "moments" when God
is alive and vivid in new and stimulating
experiences that are beyond explanation other
than — "that's God". Loving relationships,
friendships, the beauty of nature, the complex-
ities of life and the universe; not to mention
music, poetry and the conscience of man: all
speak of God. History is full of holy men who
carry the message: God is love and He is to
be discovered in our love of self and others.

*God, known and yet incomprehensible, help me to
discover You in my doubts and confusions.*

*"I haven't understood a bar of music in my life,
but I have felt it."*

Igor Stravinsky

It is okay not to "understand".

A miracle is not to be understood but experienced. So much in life we will never understand and there is growth in confusion. We are not perfect. We will never be perfect. The mystery of life is exactly that — a mystery.

As an alcoholic I often sought to appear "as God". I had to have an answer for everything, even if I made up the answer! Not to know was humiliating for me because it took away control, my need to be in charge, my hopeless and exhausting quest for perfection. With the failure to be perfect came the guilt, shame and anger.

Today I am able to live with life's daily confusions — and it's okay!

*Lord, help me never to lose touch with the feelings
that keep me human.*

*"Extremists think that 'communication' means
agreeing with them."*

Leo Rosten

As an alcoholic I was an extremist. I was
not only compulsive and obsessive about
alcohol, but I became compulsive and obsessive
about my opinions, my thoughts and my
attitude towards life. Anybody who disagreed
with me was wrong or a fool! I only listened
to those who were saying what I wanted to
hear.

For years I played at being God. But that
spiritual part of me, that I believe exists in all
of us, was isolated and unhappy with this
behavior. Although I would never admit it, I
knew that often I was wrong, bull-headed and
in pain. I would spend sleepless nights thinking
how I could say I was sorry without apologizing!
For years my pride and ego kept me sick and
unhappy.

Today I appreciate those who have a different view on life. Today I can disagree with my
neighbor without carrying a grudge. Today I
can live with difference.

*I pray that I may always hear what my opponent
is saying.*

"If Negro freedom is taken away, or that of any minority group, the freedom of all the people is taken away."

Paul Robeson

As a recovering alcoholic I belong to a minority. As somebody with the disease of addiction I am aware of my difference. And I have experienced prejudice and injustice because I was not born like other people.

But in a spiritual sense the acceptance of my disease has given me a freedom that unites me with other minorities, other "different" groups, the countless shades of humanity. My disease has produced a spiritual unity and bond with creation that makes me rejoice in my difference and produces a tolerance of others that was not there before. In this sense I thank God for my dis-ease.

You, who made the different, also created the unity; help me find both in my life.

"To teach men how to live without certainty and yet without being paralyzed by hesitation is perhaps the chief thing philosophy can do."
                                    Bertrand Russell

I suppose the "Twelve Steps" are a practical philosophy of how to live positively with the disease of alcoholism: (a) Don't drink. (b) Find a God in your life that is understandable. (c) Begin to make positive choices in attitudes and behaviors. (d) Let "never forget" be an essential part of the message.

The miracle of this philosophy is that it reaches out to so many who suffer with addictive compulsions and teaches us how to live with being imperfect. I believe the Twelve Steps are the answer to "The Fall" of man — we are going home to God.

Let me see beyond the logic to Your loving energy.

*"The aim of education is the knowledge not of fact,
but of values."*
                        Dean William R. Inge

Facts can sometimes confuse. They can be used to hide behind. They can be manipulated into lies. Facts are no substitute for values — human values.

Today I not only value my life but I value life itself. When I walk amongst nature, I taste her purity, observe her beauty, experience her strength — and I know I am a part of it all. Today my values have changed because I see myself as "part of" rather than "separate from". I belong to this universe, this world, this planet and what I do affects the essential value of life. With my daily respect for self comes a respect for property, people, different cultures and God.

Today the things I truly value I do not pay for; the things I cherish cannot be won or bought. Spirituality is free.

*Teach me to value the meaning of freedom and the
richness of life.*

"Treat the other man's faith gently; it is all he has to believe with."

Henry Hoskins

I said that I was a nonviolent drunk. Today I am able to see that I was sarcastic and verbally violent, and this was no less painful or destructive to the victim. A target for my anger and venom was the faith and beliefs of others, especially when they differed radically from my own. My alcoholism made me a prejudiced and bigoted man, a prisoner of my arrogance.

My sobriety teaches me to be accepting and tolerant of the views and opinions of others. A spirituality that embraces all men — rather than a narrow and restrictive religion — is my prescription for life. I have exchanged bigotry for freedom, and I am happy in God's world.

I pray that my acceptance of my fellow man, regardless of culture or creed, may lead to understanding.

"The fault is in us."
                              Hannah Arendt

As a drunk I would blame everybody for my problems: My family was too controlling. I did not have people around who understood me. I worked too hard and the people were too demanding. The weather was awful!

Today I accept my involvement with my past predicament. Bad things happened to me because I created them in my life. And this means that good and creative things can also happen in my life if I create them. I need not remain the problem. I can be the solution!

Let me discover Your answer in my response to life.

*"Few people are capable of expressing with
equanimity, opinions which differ from the
prejudices of their social environment."*
                                   Albert Einstein

Part of my growth in sobriety is learning to
say "no". For years as a practicing alcoholic
I tried to please everybody with the result that
I pleased very few and became exhausted in
the process! I have learned that sometimes I
need to be unpopular in order to remain sober;
unpopular to remain serene; unpopular to
practice my spiritual program.

To understand the gift of God's creation
requires the acceptance that we are not the
same and, as people, we will have different
opinions and attitudes. Truth has many shades.
To be unpopular at times is reality; truth is
always real.

*I pray that I might always say and do what I
believe to be right, regardless of public opinion.*

"You cannot build a reputation on things you are going to do."

Mabel Newcomber

Procrastination is the addicts' game. I will give up alcohol tomorrow. Soon I will take an inventory of my eating habits. Later I will talk to him about my anger and pain. Tomorrow and tomorrow — but it never happens!

The tragedy is that we not only bring pain and problems into our lives but we keep them there. Recovery requires action; sobriety and the spiritual program demand movement.

Today I will talk about my pain.

*"Creative intelligence in its various forms and
activities is what makes man."*
James Harvey Robinson

Spirituality is being a positive and creative
human being in all areas of my life; this I know
to be true today. I am not only creative, I am
a creative human being. God created me to
create. I am a part of His love for the world;
through me great and wonderful events can
happen. Although I am not divine, I know that
I share divinity. I am special.

But with this knowledge comes tremendous
responsibility because things are only going to
happen if I make them happen in my life. To
know that I am creative does not make me
creative. I have to do something, make something, create something in my life.

Today I work at my life like a carpenter
works at his wood. I chip away those things
I do not want; I smooth down the rough areas
of my life, and I polish up those things I want
people to see. I accept responsibility for my
creativity, and I thank God, on a daily basis,
for it.

*Teach me, O Creator of the universe, to use my
life as a tool for goodness, joy and truth.*

> *"Gluttony is not a secret vice."*
> *Orson Welles*

The unspoken disease of food: hide in food, bury anger with food, cry behind food. Food addiction — eating, forever dieting, starving — is the hidden disease that is becoming more obvious. But are we talking about it? Recovering alcoholics minimize it and get lost in ice cream and doughnuts. For many people the pain around food is as real as alcohol or any other drug. And the family and relationships suffer.

Today I am willing to talk about it. Spirituality affects all my life and this involves my eating habits and body weight. God does not make junk and so I choose not to eat junk. Today I choose to talk about the buried emotions that I am stuffing behind the food. That is a step towards living.

When I bless the food at meal time, may I also bless my abstinence.

*"Treat all men alike. Give them all the same
laws. Give them all an even chance to live
and grow."*

Chief Joseph

Today it is important for me to remember
that I am not the only human being in this
universe; I need to respect and be considerate
of others. Spirituality requires that I treat all
people with dignity and respect because they
carry something of God within them — the
image of God is with all men. In this way I
show and give respect to self.

As an alcoholic I was selfish and demanding,
wanting my way all the time. Sobriety teaches
me that "the way" must include others; my
fellow men are part of my life and journey.
I cannot live in isolation and be sober.

*O Spirit of the World, teach me to respect all men
as a service to myself.*

"One person with a belief is equal to a force of ninety-nine who have only interests."
                                    John Stuart Mill

I believe in sobriety because it works for me. I believe in sobriety because it makes me feel good about myself. I believe in sobriety because it has enabled me to rejoin the human race; I was so tired of feeling lonely, ashamed and isolated.

Also this belief I have in me has rekindled a positive relationship with my higher power. Today God is a friend. Today I understand more about what He wants for me. Today I am broad enough in my thinking to find God in anything that is positive and creative — from music to hugs in the park!

Belief has developed with my spiritual program, and I am able to face the daily pains and conflicts of life. Today I know what it is to be a winner — and, thank God, it doesn't mean I have to be perfect or in control. My total belief in God and self enables me to love me through my failings.

Master of the beliefs of all men, thank You for the gift of my believing in myself.

"The price of freedom of religion or of speech or of the press is that we must put up with, and even pay for, a good deal of rubbish."

                        Justice Robert Jackson

I need to be tolerant in my sobriety. I need to allow others to say what they feel and live according to their standards.

I was intolerant towards people who were different from myself. Much of what I criticized yesterday, I accept today; some things I still reject.

To love a person should not require "sameness"; equally, I can accept a person without agreeing with what they say or how they behave. Disagreements and conflicts lead to growth; change requires a variety of forces.

Not everything I say or do is "pure" — and that has become the key to the acceptance of others. My history teaches me that I benefit from the variety of opinions that are represented in mankind.

Lord, You have created many ways to Truth, may I appreciate them through the experiences of others.

"Poetry is not an assertion of truth, but the making of that truth more fully real to us."
T. S. Eliot

God is able to communicate Himself in a thousand different ways and one such way is poetry.

Spirituality is discovering God in His creation, and this involves more than religion or denominationalism. Spirituality is a comprehensive approach to God's world and is the unifying factor at the center of the universe. Spirituality is about what is true — wherever it is found in the world.

Poetry and other art forms become part of the spiritual journey for us as we struggle to understand and communicate truth.

In poetry may I find an expression of Your love for me; in my use of poetry, may I express my love for You.

"Sleep that knots up the ravelled sleave of care."
William Shakespeare

When I was new in my recovery from alcoholism I was told to remember the letters H.A.L.T.: Do not get too: Hungry, Angry, Lonely or Tired.

Sleep is something my body needs, and even if I do not always know it, my body does. The tiredness in my body is telling me to slow down. Sleep is part of my spiritual program because it enables me to feel rested, invigorated and alive. Through sleep I am able to be creative and positive in my life — showing a practical love to my body. Sleep is me taking care of self!

Thank You for the joy and rest that comes
with sleep.

"Too many people are thinking of security instead of opportunity; they seem more afraid of life than death."
                                        James Byrnes

Today I am aware of the opportunities that I did not recognize when I was drinking. Drinking stopped me from seeing the life that was before me. I drank myself away from the daily miracle. I missed the sunsets, the fun of relationships, the joy of the theater and the satisfaction of being "aware".

In the business world I did not see the opportunity for profit and expansion; I did not create or have faith in my ideas, and I was not able to understand or absorb the new information to be successful in my life. Alcoholism kept me on the outside of my life.

Today I am alive in my life, creating, expanding and enjoying my leisure. With sobriety I have the opportunity to experience God in the many aspects of life.

Teach me to find You in the risks of life.

*"Honesty is the first chapter of the book
of wisdom."*

Thomas Jefferson

It is impossible to have a spiritual program
without being honest. It is impossible to be
recovering from addiction without being
honest. An aspect of sobriety is honesty.

Today I can see that I was never really
known when I was "using" because I was so
dishonest. I stopped other people from getting
to know me. I stopped me from getting to know
me. Part of my pain involved my dishonesty;
part of my loneliness and feelings of isolation
was caused by my dishonesty; the unmanageability that nearly destroyed my life grew in
my dishonesty.

Today I need to be honest, rigorously honest
— even in the small things. I can no longer
exist to please others — I need to please myself.
I need to love myself by being honest.

*O God of wisdom, let me find truth in the honesty
of my own life.*

"The ablest men in all walks of modern life are men of faith."

Bruce Barton

It is important for those of us who have been crushed by the disease of addiction to have faith that life will get better. We stopped "using" or being co-dependent because the behavior was destroying us. Our lives were disintegrating in negative behavior and attitudes. Now we have chosen a different way to live.

Today I seek to find God in my freedom of choice, my ability to change. I have faith in the daily belief that my life will get better so long as I avoid those things that hurt me. My faith enables me to change.

O God, my faith in me reflects my belief in You.

"Sexual pleasure, wisely used and not abused, may prove the stimulus and liberator of our finest and most exalted activities."

Havelock Ellis

Sex is most beautiful because it enables the human being to experience and give love at an intimate and personal level. It also combines all the spiritual senses of body, mind and feeling in one expression, balancing tenderness with strength, patience with desire, need with selflessness.

Also the awareness and experience of a beautiful sexuality should be taken into all other manifestations of life — work, leisure, friendship, sports and prayer.

The gift of sex is one of our finest and most creative attributes and leads to all that is noble in man, therefore, it should not be used irresponsibly. Today I understand that I have a responsibility to the gifts that God has shared with me.

May I find in my sexuality an awareness of You.

"Education today, more than ever before, must see clearly the dual objectives: education for living and education for making a living."
James Mason Wood

The spiritual life is a productive life. Not only does it make for a prosperous life in every sense of the word but it makes for a creative lifestyle. Nothing is wasted on the spiritual man; he learns from his mistakes and doubts.

For too long I was stunted in my spiritual growth by negative and destructive thinking. I became dependent upon a sick self and attracted equally sick people. I used my education and knowledge to keep people out and remained isolated. I needed to change. I wanted to change. But how? As with everything else in life I needed to imitate those who were successful. I needed to be shown how to live a different way. I needed to discover the power of my spirituality. I found successful people. They helped me. Today I am able to help myself.

I pray for the knowledge to imitate those who are successful in life.

"Success is a journey not a destination."
                    Ben Sweetland

So long as I am sober I know that I am successful. But I also know that my sobriety is more than keeping away from the first drink. My sobriety requires that I be a creative and successful human being in all areas of my life — in my relationships, at work, with my family, my business ventures and in my acts of charity. The road to success is exactly that — it is a "road" that I am traveling along, and I will be on it until the day I die. I suppose the danger is in thinking that I have arrived. Then I get complacent and apathetic, I slow down and the energy for recovery is diminished.

Today I know that I am successful so long as I keep moving along with my spiritual program.

*Let me always be confident as I walk in my
journey of life.*

"Treat people as if they were what they ought to be, and you help them to become what they are capable of being."
                              Johann W. von Goethe

My program of recovery from alcoholism helps me have a relationship with myself and helps me relate to and understand others. The more I understand my strengths and weaknesses, the more I am able to understand others.

Any understanding of spirituality involves other people. If spirituality helps me become what God intends for me, then this is also true for others. Today I choose to treat myself and other people as children of God, remembering that we were created to reach for the skies!

Lord, our potential forever rests in You.

*"We have the power to make this the best
generation of mankind in the history of the world
— or to make it the last."*
                                    John F. Kennedy

War is tragic because it always destroys; it
kills creation itself. People, buildings, relationships, trust, hope, culture, history, youth —
they all disappear behind a puff of smoke. The
immensity of war is such that it cannot be fully
comprehended. Only isolated aspects can be
understood: a child is maimed, a treaty is
broken, a race is blamed, bullets are heard and
a history that existed within a human life is
ended in silence.

Addiction is a kind of war — a silent war
that exists within an individual and family.
People, trust, buildings, hope, culture, history
and youth disappear behind a glass or a pill.
Creation is attacked from the inside; God is
forgotten in an act of destructive selfishness.

Teach me to make peace in my life.

*"We have just enough religion to make us hate,
but not enough to make us love one another."*
                                        Jonathan Swift

Religion is a powerful influence in the world, but so often the "power" is negative. It has been used to judge, divide, separate and control people; rob them of their freedom and creativity; chain them to creeds and teachings that are not comprehensible. Unfortunately, religion has become dull and lifeless for many people and God's love is missed.

But the power of creative spirituality is alive in God's world. It unites and frees the people so that they can be discovered in their individuality. Difference is accepted, choice is respected and healing is perceived in our ability to love.

*Let me ever bring the gift of God's spirituality to
those who have misplaced it.*

"We work to become, not to acquire."
Elbert Hubbard

I believe it is easier to get well than it is to stay sick — but we must be prepared to work for our sobriety. We need to confront the disease and discover the "person" that God created. The road to recovery is rewarding because we cast aside those aspects of our character that have been destroying us and discover our strengths, virtues and God-given spirituality.

For years I worked for money or for security or for acclaim — today I am working on myself for myself. I work at discovering God in His world, and I am also finding God in my life. I realize that my creative work coincides with God's will for the world.

Thank You for the gift of work that enables me to
discover more of me.

> *"There are three kinds of lies, lies, damned*
> *lies and statistics."*
> *Benjamin Disraeli*

I used to be able to hide behind anything — even statistics. Figures, and the quoting of figures, can expand the ego and keep you sick. They can confuse the issues by making everything complicated.

In the field of alcoholism statistics are important for comparison and research but they can never be a substitute for a "rigorous honesty" that is based upon personal experience. I do not think that statistics alone stopped a person from drinking, but the sharing of a personal suffering and victory can produce an identification that leads to change.

As a recovering alcoholic I need to know the statistics concerning my disease but I also need to know that today's recovery is based upon yesterday's honest sharing.

Let me always see the faces behind the numbers.

> *"The brighter you are, the more you have*
> *to learn."*
>
> *Don Herold*

The one thing I know in sobriety is how much I do not know! I thought I knew everything about God because I was a priest, only to discover that I had made Him a prisoner of the Church. Once I was willing to free Him from my prison, I discovered a freedom and awareness that daily fascinates and astounds me.

Today I see that the glory of God shines within my pain, within my loneliness, within my confusion, and the acceptance of my disease is the key to recovery. Today the suffering enables me to discover a realistic spirituality — and it is okay to be confused!

With each new day, Lord, let me learn something
— even if it is that I have not learned anything
that day!

*"Capital, as such, is not evil; it is its wrong use
that is evil."*
                        Mohandas K. Gandhi

Today I am not afraid to say that I am
concerned for my prosperity — not just in
terms of health, friendship and employment
but also concerning money. For years I was
concerned to have the best, buy the best, own
the best and not "shortchange" myself — yet
I felt guilty in having such feelings. Today in
my sobriety I truly believe that I deserve the
best. In this way I am loving myself. Money,
prosperity and capital are not "bad" in themselves; it is how we use them.

Today, as promised in my recovery, things
are certainly getting better and I am able to
invest and buy wisely. Some years ago I would
squander money on my addiction. Today I am
able to appreciate and share my monetary
benefits. Family, friends and the "needy" can
genuinely share my prosperity: the more I give
away today, the more I get.

*Thank You for all the many benefits You have
showered upon me in my recovery,
not least capital. May I always
use it responsibly.*

*"Christ cannot possibly have been a Jew. I don't
have to prove that scientifically. It is a fact!"*
                                        Joseph Goebbels

Today I know that if a lie is said loudly
enough, often enough, with ceremony and
ritual, people will believe it. I can identify with
the above statement: I said I was not alcoholic
because I did not drink every day, in the
mornings, all day and I was too young! People
believed me. Some people still choose to believe
this lie.

Spirituality requires that I not only confront
the lies in other people but also in myself.
Usually if I am angry at the remarks of others,
it is because they remind me of myself. Today
I seek not simply to condemn but to understand.

*May I continue to learn from the criticism I make
of others.*

"In every child who is born, under no matter what circumstances, and of no matter what parents, the potentiality of the human race is born again."
                                                    James Agee

Today I am able to believe and see the God-given dignity of the human race in the faces and lifestyles of others. In the challenge and rebelliousness of youth is the hope for tomorrow.

Today I can associate myself with the need to question, risk and "be outrageous". Today I can play, laugh at myself and own my craziness. Today I do not need to be perfect.

When I used drugs, I was so judgmental, serious and controlling. Everything had to have a place, or an answer, or be acceptable to others. My moments of guilt were caused by my inability to please others.

Today I can be childlike and identify with the radical message for tomorrow: "to thine own self be true!"

I see a child looking at the stars and I smile; I am that child.

*"The hopeful man sees success where others see
failure, sunshine where others see shadows
and storm."*

O. S. Marden

Spirituality involves our attitudes and perceptions as well as our prayers. Spirituality requires a realistic awareness of what we need and what we have been given. Spirituality sees beyond the problems into the solution.

Hope is a feeling that is based on a spiritual perception of life that shuns apathy and negativity. Everything can be used for good if it is perceived realistically; destructive experiences, painful moments and failed relationships can all be used to create a new tomorrow.

The hope that stems from our ability to change requires a realistic understanding of what has happened. No aspect of life should be wasted because it can point to a glorious tomorrow.

*Teach me to discover the secret of success in the
problems of life.*

*"Love your neighbor as thyself, but choose
your neighbor."*

Louise Beal

Part of my recovery and sobriety involves change. It is not enough to "put down the jug" to gain sobriety; I need to make substantial changes in my life.

Where I live, with whom I live, the friends I keep and the relationships I make are crucial to my sobriety. Human beings imitate. They imitate clothes, hairstyles and mannerisms. Sobriety is also imitated.

As a recovering alcoholic, I can only be spiritually happy with those who are joyous and free; I need to find them.

God, You are to be found in Your creation. Let me seek You in a noble lifestyle.

*"Nothing is more terrible than activity
without insight."*
                              Thomas Carlyle

I believe that recovery can only begin when
we "see" or start to get a glimpse of who we
are and what we are dealing with . . . insight;
an insight into self.

However, the moment we begin to see must
be followed by a determined effort to discover
more; digging through the denial, pain and
manipulation to the disease. Then after discovering the disease in our lives, we must be
prepared to risk talking about it — on a daily
basis.

Recovery requires a daily desire to see,
discover and talk about our addiction — with
this insight comes recovery.

*You are the light of the world; shine through
my honesty.*

"When a man has pity on all living creatures,
then only is he noble."

Buddha

We all need each other. More than this, we need to help and sustain each other. And this concept extends beyond human beings — the world is full of other creatures that God has made and which make our lives so fascinating and entertaining. Animals and plants make up our ecological history and yet so often we rob and hurt our environment.

Recovery from alcoholism means more than putting down "the drink". Today I am picking up a responsible attitude that makes me care, on a spiritual level, for my world.

Lord, as I look around my world I cannot help but
worship You.

*"Freedom comes from human beings, rather than
from laws and institutions."*
                                    Clarence Darrow

The disease of alcoholism does not live in
bottles or books. It lives in people. Drug
problems are people problems. Sobriety exists
in the man, not the theory.

In this sense recovery must be experienced,
rather than simply talked about. The Program
is essentially not written in books or taught
in lecture rooms but is lived in the lives of
people; the program stems from the heart of
man.

I believe the program is that spark of divinity
that God has bestowed upon all of us — and
we must discover it within.

*Teach me to remember that to think a smile
without revealing a smile is to be grumpy.*

*"It is the chiefest point of happiness that man is
willing to be what he is."*
Desiderius Erasmus

I am an alcoholic. Today I am able to love
myself because I am able to accept myself.

More than this: because I am able to accept
myself, I am able to be myself. The acceptance
of my disease around alcohol has taught me
that I am not perfect, and I do not live in
a perfect world — this leads to an acceptance
of others. My pain around alcohol has given
me an insight into the sufferings of others —
and this has produced spiritual growth.

I am happy not because I am an alcoholic
but because I know that I am an alcoholic.
Today I can be what I was meant to be, rather
than the "fake" that I was becoming.

In the spiritual journey is the happiness.

"Let there be spaces in your togetherness."
Kahlil Gibran

As an alcoholic I demanded love and was possessive of others. I had a selfish love that treated people as "things" — for my own satisfaction and survival. I was claustrophobic in my affection and smothered any creative love; my fear of being alone made me blackmail people with my needs and emotions.

Today I can love people while still allowing them to breathe. An important part of my program is detachment; I take responsibility for me and I allow others to take responsibility for themselves. I give the people I love space.

Sometimes I need to love a person enough to let them go. Spiritually I am beginning to understand that in order to be free, I must give freedom to others.

God, in the "spaces" of my love is the growth experienced.

"I am a man; nothing human is alien to me."
                                              Terence

Humility is not so much about trying to be "good" as accepting that I am imperfect. For too long I thought that humility was "keeping the peace", appearing to be "perfect", bottling up my anger and resentments — living a life of "people-pleasing".

Today I understand that humility is being real. It is accepting my humanity and being honest in my relationships. Humility is respecting the lives of others but also respecting my own. Humility is seeking to reveal that divinity that God has given to my life. Humility is knowing that in the lives of my fellow man — the good and the bad — is me.

Master, let me have the humility to be real.

*"The Bible tells us to love our neighbors and also
to love our enemies; probably because they are
generally the same people."*
                                        G. K. Chesterton

The spiritual program that I embrace makes
me look to where I am, rather than where I
want to be. I must live in the now, rather than
the never-never-land of tomorrow.

To love my world I need to seek to understand those people who live in my world. To
love my world involves an acceptance of those
who are different from me. I must seek to build
bridges, rather than barriers. It is so easy for
me to talk about loving and being concerned
for the starving millions and forgetting to love
and relate to the typist in my office or the
neighbor down the street.

I have some experience of people who can
be difficult because I lived with the addicted
me for many years; I am the key to my enemies.

*Teach me to accept in love those who, for today, I
do not like.*

*"But one day when I was sitting quiet and feeling
like a motherless child, which I was, it came to me
that feeling of being part of everything,
not separate at all. I knew that if I cut a tree,
my arm would bleed."*
                              Alice Walker

Today I am aware of the truth that I belong.
I am an essential part of God's world. I share
divinity because God made me. Today I choose
to seek that spiritual center in me that is
forever positive and creative. Today I am the
center of my universe.

Past hurts and wrongs cannot take away the
uniqueness in my life. Past abuses and painful
put-downs, my years of alternating between the
lost child and the scapegoat in my family need
not make me a victim today. Today I am free
to choose recovery and an acceptance of self.
Today I choose to associate with the winners
of this world. Today I participate in creation
by being a creative person for me. Yesterday's
pain need not have any power in my life today.

*When I kneel before the stream, mountains and
stars, I feel me.*

"The life of the law has not been logic; it has been experience."
                    Oliver Wendell Holmes, Jr.

Today I respect the law. In this way I respect the society in which I live. I am not "an island unto myself". I live in a community and have a responsibility to myself and that community — such is sobriety.

For years I did what I wanted and tried not to be "found out". I was manipulative, dishonest and unhappy; to stay sick is depressing and exhausting.

Then I decided to remove the pain. I accepted the disease and began to "change" my life. I discovered the "spiritual law" of freedom with responsibility. Law is the collective experience of the many who choose to live a certain way, and today I choose to live amongst them. My understanding of spirituality involves respecting the laws that give me the dignity of citizenship.

O Lord, help me to see that in the laws of civilization is the gift of freedom.

*"The chief cause of human errors is to be found in
the prejudices picked up in childhood."*
                                        Rene Descartes

During the past few years I have begun to
recognize how many of my prejudices were
planted in childhood. Family, teachers, priests
and "the neighborhood" passed on to me
prejudices: "The Jews are bad because they
killed Jesus." "Blacks are inferior to white
people — but you should be kind to them."
"Women should obey the man of the house."
"Gays are child molesters." "People who do
not accept Jesus will not go to Heaven." "Sex
is for having babies and you should not enjoy
it."

Today I live with the problem of knowing
that these statements are untrue but a part
of me is still affected by them.

Today my spiritual program demands that I
expose prejudice for the "hate-mail" that it is,
and try to pass on to the next generation the
joy that comes from love, acceptance and
freedom.

Let the children grow in freedom.

*"Going to Church doesn't make you a Christian
any more than going to the garage makes you
a car."*

Laurence J. Peter

I cannot help but believe that the truth of Christianity is about bringing the world and mankind together, rather than creating divisions and resentments. It must be much bigger than what we do or say in any building. Christ's truth seeks to discover God in the splendor of His varied world. In this sense, Christianity is an aspect of the world's spirituality!

My addiction made me a small man with a small god. Constantly focusing on the differences in the world stopped me from seeing the glaring similarities; my exclusiveness kept me a lonely man. The world of black and white, rather than shades of creative color, is a sick and dangerous world to live in. Jesus Christ reveals for me the "man for others"; the bridge by which reconciliation and harmony can be achieved. His message for me is not so much a series of dogmas as a revealed journey into Truth.

*In the created stranger, help me to discover
the friend.*

"Only work which is the product of inner compulsion can have spiritual meaning."
                              Walter Gropius

I have developed, in my recovery, an awareness of the beauty of this world and an appreciation of what man can produce. Sobriety has made art accessible. Today I can see beauty in paintings, sculpture, music, literature and the natural "art" of nature.

Spirituality is always creative and it is at the center of all that is good, noble and inspiring. Although I am not an artist, I can appreciate and have a feeling of "belonging" to the beauty of this world — in a sense it all happens and takes shape through me. The rediscovery of spirituality has brought the world and the universe into my life.

Help me to have the desire to recreate Your splendors through my experiences.

*"For us, patriotism is the same as the love
of humanity."*
                              Mohandas Gandhi

Today I am on the side of mankind. I am
convinced that my welfare is generated by the
peace and stability of the world. The love and
joy that produces spiritual growth stems from
my relationships in the world: we cannot exist
alone.

Today I strive to bring the world and people
together; we must not seek to be the same but
rather rejoice in the richness of difference.

Drugs always divide, separate and isolate;
spirituality unites. Today I am an optimist for
mankind because of what has happened in my
own life.

Thank You for a humanity that can be shared.

"I was a free-thinker before I knew how to think."
George Bernard Shaw

All of us are influenced by somebody. Not to be influenced is to remain an ignorant person. Most of us hinder our thinking, particularly around spiritual things, because of pride. We don't like change. We find it hard to accept attitudes and opinions that differ from our own. Pride keeps us deaf and often stupid. However, the daily program of a lived spirituality encourages a variety of opinions and attitudes. We can learn from different customs, lifestyles and religions. We can be helped in our understanding of life by the stranger.

I know that I do not have all the answers. Perhaps you carry my answers. Today I am prepared to listen to you.

God, the sustainer of all religions and
philosophies, help us to discover You
in our differences.

*"Wherever two people meet, there are really six
people present. There is each man as he sees
himself, each man as the other person sees him,
and each man as he really is."*
                    William James

Part of my spiritual journey involves the
discovery of "self". For years I pretended to
be what I was not; for years I pretended to
be what I imagined myself to be; for years I
pretended to be what you wanted me to be
— always my real "self" eluded me.

Today I am beginning to know myself. I know
my needs. I understand my strengths. I accept
my weaknesses and I live with my confusions.
From the time I decided to put down the glass
of alcohol, it progressively got better — but
there is still a great deal I do not understand.
Man's inhumanity to man, the daily violence
and suffering, my own personal greed, cowardice and arrogance — where does it come from?
I don't know and today that is okay. However,
I still search; my suspicion is that the answer
lies within my own insecurities.

*In Your time, Master, may I grow in
my understanding of self.*

"The child without ambition is like a watch with a broken spring."

R. W. Stockman

It is not wrong to have ambition. It is not wrong to want to be "somebody". The tragedy is that this has to be said!

For too long we have played the tapes in our head that discouraged ambition and creative pride. We confused humility with timidity and self-abuse. We waited for things to happen, rather than made them happen.

Today I know that I am a creature of God — created to create. God is at work in my life. I am part of His miracle for the world.

O God, may I always have ambition for those things that are good and true.

"Each honest calling, each walk of life, has its own elite, its own aristocracy based upon excellence of performance."

James Bryant Conant

Everybody has a gift and a special feature that is unique to themselves. Unfortunately so many people are so busy admiring the gifts of others that they miss their own; they are so caught up in the lives of others that they miss the "specialness" of their own existence. One of the symptoms of my alcoholism was low self-esteem. Of course I acted a role of confidence. I pretended that everything was okay. I wore the mask of success — but deep within myself, I was always waiting for the world to find out that I was a fake, that something was missing in my life.

In recovery I have discovered God's powerful gift of spirituality and I know that through my life a uniqueness exists in the world. I have the capacity to make the day better — not only for myself but also for others.

Thank You for the "specialness" of my life.

*"To treat your facts with imagination is one thing,
but to imagine your facts is another."*
                                        John Burroughs

When I was drinking, I was always confusing
fantasy with reality. Lies got mingled with the
facts and the facts became exaggerated. It was
almost impossible for me to distinguish between
reality and fantasy, imagination and fact. My
life was a complicated lie.

Today I have a program of "rigorous"
honesty; I must be rigorous and stop the game
before it starts. I need to practice the principles
of recovery in every area of my life. The
spiritual road involves a comprehensive journey
and nothing need be left out.

*God, who created the mountains, help me to take
responsibility for the grit between my toes.*

"He that is without sin amongst you, let him cast the first stone."

Jesus Christ

It is so easy for me to focus on the failings of others and miss my own. My attraction to gossip is that it is usually about other people and that keeps the attention away from me. Sometimes I am made to "feel good" by exposing the weaknesses of others.

This attitude needs to be changed if I am ever to fully enjoy the fruits of sobriety. I do not need to be drinking to behave like a drunk; gossip and character assassination are reminiscent of my past addictive behavior. I do not need the side of me that seeks to destroy the character of others. With my spiritual program, I am trying to change.

May I grow in my forgiveness and acceptance of others.

Forgiveness
is the key
to action
and
freedom.

Hannah Arendt

*"Understanding is the reward of faith. Therefore
seek not to understand that thou mayest believe,
but believe that thou mayest understand."*
                                        Saint Augustine

Today I understand that God is love and that
it makes more sense to live my life with love
than with anger, resentment and despair. I
know that the answer to life, with all the
problems that may arise, is love. Not simply
loving those people who love me, but beginning
to love and understand those who dislike or
hate me. Being imperfect people in an imperfect world produces enemies. Today I love my
world by listening to my critics, changing
unreasonable attitudes, growing in the humility
that comes from silence. Change is part of
God's blessing of love.

This I believe. This I understand. And step
by step it is beginning to work in my life.

*May my love for the world give me
an understanding of self.*

"Men of integrity, by their very existence, rekindle the belief that as a people we can live above the level of moral squalor."
                                    John Gardner

I understand integrity to be a willingness to make sacrifices for what we believe to be true. The living of a spiritual program must lead to integrity.

Not so many years ago integrity was not an understood word in my vocabulary because of my unwillingness to make sacrifices. I was so selfishly preoccupied with my "wants" that I gave little thought to the needs of others. The more I lost myself in "self", the greater was the emotional pain.

Today I live the paradox that it is only in giving that I truly receive.

May I daily express the paradox of sacrifice in my life.

"The principal mark of genius is not perfection but originality, the opening of new frontiers."
                                        Arthur Koestler

I need to remember that genius is often simplicity itself. The original thought need not be abstract, intellectual or technical; the thought exists to transmit the message.

In the slogans "Keep it Simple", "One Day at a Time", "Don't Pick up the First Drink", wisdom combines with simplicity to produce sobriety. God is at work outside of His church and the spiritual message always brings healing. A.A. is more than a "fellowship of genius", it is divinity set to a program. What began with a group of alcoholics will cross new frontiers into the healing of the world.

Lord of Truth, let us always be open and receptive to Your voice.

"The hottest places in Hell are reserved for those, who in time of great moral crises, maintain their neutrality."

Dante Alighieri

Each human being makes a personal Hell here on earth. Often we do it not by what we perpetrate but in what we allow to happen. So much of the loneliness and isolation that many addicts and their families experience is caused by them remaining hidden and silent. The pretense that everything is okay is not only untrue but deadly. Silence and compliance kills more addicts than a thousand needles!

Today I choose not to be neutral in my life. I speak about my alcoholism so that I can on a daily basis make war on the disease that nearly killed me. I speak out about the disease of addiction so that society cannot say that it did not know what was happening. I speak up for treatment and recovery because I know it can work in the vast majority of cases. I am not neutral when it comes to addiction because I am fighting for my life.

God, give me the courage to speak up in the crowd; let me live the message I was privileged to receive.

"Without freedom, no one really has a name."
Milton Acorda

Part of my identity involves my disease. I am an alcoholic and my name is . . . And with this recognition of who I am comes the liberty and freedom to live and create in God's world. Who I am involves what I am; in the fusion of the two is my spiritual identity.

For years I ran from myself because I wanted to be different. I felt that I would not be acceptable or good enough for you. In running from me, I lost my identity; the seed of low self-esteem was sown.

With the spiritual recognition that I can only be who I am came the freedom of existence and identity. I am what I am!

Lord, You said once, "I am who I am."
Well, so am I!

"Hypocrisy: prejudice with a halo."
                                    Ambrose Bierce

As a religious person I could be such a hypocrite. I thought that my "goodness" was dependent upon my judging others to be inferior. I was always putting other people down so that I could appear terrific.

But a part of me always knew this was wrong. I ignored the religious teaching that emphasized forgiveness and acceptance and instead focused on judgment and condemnation. It was all part of my sickness. Inside I was hurting and feeling guilty but I hid these feelings with a mask of hypocrisy and respectability.

Today I do not need to do this. I have a religion that can accept the non-religious and rejoice in the different cultures and creeds. I do not fear those who are different, and I am slowly beginning to accept my many imperfections.

You, who have loved me through forgiveness,
help me to forgive.

*"An idealist is one who, on noticing that a rose
smells better than a cabbage, concludes that it will
also make better soup."*

H. L. Mencken

The spiritual program teaches me to be an
idealist with my feet on the ground. People will
continue to hurt, get angry and tell lies;
wrestling with imperfection is not just my
problem. I need to accept that I live in an
imperfect world and recovery involves reality,
not illusion.

My responsibility in recovery is for my life.
I cannot change other people, events or
relationships — I can only change me. I am
not God. Each time I forget this fact, I risk
another hurt.

*Help me to aspire for ideals that are within
my grasp.*

"Sixty years ago I knew everything; now I know nothing; education is a progressive discovery of our own ignorance."

Will Durant

Spirituality is the art of knowing that we do not know. It is waking up in the morning with our eyes fully opened and awaiting the adventure of the new day. New things, new theories, new facts are being discovered every day and it makes for a glorious, confusing and exciting world.

There was a time when I could not say this; a time when knowledge and facts were collected and regurgitated. I used knowledge to protect myself from the challenge and inconsistencies of life. God had to be not only a proven fact but evidenced in theories and dogmas — the mystery was lost.

Today I believe that God cannot be contained by dogma and rules. The doubts have become part of my faith. The state of "not knowing" becomes creative and stimulating. My relationship with God today is real. To "not know" is the beginning of wisdom.

You, who have spoken through the wind and the fire, speak through my doubts.

"Not he who has little, but he who wishes more,
is poor."
                    Seneca (4 B. C. — A. D. 65)

In my recovery I must still deal with that compulsive side of my nature that always wants more.

I forget to be grateful for what I have. I ruin relationships because I have a code of behavior that I expect from others but not myself. I miss the fun of the moment because I am preoccupied with what I am missing elsewhere. I miss the comfort of my own home as I fantasize about country mansions owned by millionaires. Always I want more — and yet in my own experience more has always been less.

Today I work hard on a spiritual program of gratitude. I have a checklist of things I need to be grateful for; I work on my disease of greed by talking about it.

Thank You for that part of me that must
remain "poor".

"We have to live today by what truth we can get today and be ready tomorrow to call it falsehood."
                                        William James

To change is to be imperfect and to be imperfect is to be wrong — at times! As an alcoholic I have a problem with ego; always wanting to be right, hating to say, "I am sorry", not wishing to appear out of control. In sobriety I must wrestle with my ego on a daily basis.

However, although I find it difficult to accept that I am imperfect, I know that I am! I know that I need to make amends. I know that I produce most of the pain in my life. Today's facts are stepping stones to tomorrow's falsehoods — and I grow with this knowledge.

Spirituality is growing in the knowledge that I do not have all the answers.

Let me experience joy and growth in the dilemmas of life.

*"In freeing people . . . our country's blessing will
also come; for profit follows righteousness."*
         Senator Albert Beveridge

Profit is more than financial benefit or
material well-being. Profit, for the recovering
alcoholic and drug addict, is being aware of life,
feeling feelings and having the capacity for a
relationship with God, self and others.

But a financial benefit is also part of spirituality; the blessing of money and financial
stability are part of God's love and trust. His
gift of freedom involves our responsibility and
stewardship of money.

With money and profit we are not only able
to have creative comforts, but we can also
make the lives of others creative. A responsible
use of money is part of my recovery program
and has become one of the joys of the "spiritual
awakening".

*Let Your blessing of money in life help me to
bless others.*

*"I have learned this at least by my experiment:
that if one advances confidently in the direction of
his dreams, and endeavors to live the life which he
has imagined, he will meet with a success
unexpected in common hours."*
                    Henry David Thoreau

Drugs brought me nightmares, never dreams.
For years I lived in fear. In the night I imagined
horrible shapes, strange colors and sounds,
experienced unspeakable tortures and awoke in
tension and sweat.

Today in sobriety my dreams are serene and
tranquil; I remember friends and loved ones
and those I most admire. I imagine God in the
beauty of His creation. He breathes His love
through me. My dreams are part of my wellness.

*God, who created men to dream their dreams, help
me to live mine.*

*"There are two ways to slide easily through life:
To believe everything or to doubt everything. Both
ways save us from thinking."*
                              Alfred Korzybski

This statement is so true for me. I was so compulsive and obsessive not only about the things that I believed in but also about the things I didn't believe in. I was extreme. Everything I did was exaggerated. I either raced through life at ten thousand miles an hour or was in neutral. Balance was absent.

Today I am developing balance in my life, more patience and more tolerance. I have discovered that my extremism was a mask by which I hid from life; I did not have to think, consider or ponder — I simply reacted.

Now I know that to believe in everything is to believe nothing; and to doubt everything is not to think. Life is "a many splendored thing" but it has a variety of options.

*God of the many, help me to discover You in the
myriad of thoughts that life produces.*

"Wine that maketh glad the heart of man."
                                        Psalm 104:15

Every good thing can be abused and alcohol is no exception. Although most people are able to enjoy the fruits of the grape and the quality of their lives are enriched by good wine, not a few are destroyed by wine! Millions of people in this world are alcoholic. They did not want to be alcoholic but they are. Their lives and relationships are destroyed by alcohol. They need to stop drinking if they are to find "gladness" in their lives. Alcoholism is a disease that cannot be cured, but it can be arrested by giving up the grape!

God can be appreciated in the grape, but He can also be experienced in the soda. We need to find new ways to be happy.

Thank You for the precious gift of choice.

"By thought I embrace the universal."
Blaise Pascal

My ability to think and communicate enables me not only to live in this world, but also to understand this world. Relationships are dependent upon me understanding my responsibilities — and when I do not think, I am usually very irresponsible.

Alcohol stopped me from thinking and behaving responsibly and created dishonesty in my life. Instead of feeling I belonged, I felt I was on the outside; instead of enjoying relationships, I was forever fighting and involved in bitter disputes; instead of enjoying the peace that comes from being a "child of God", I felt like an abandoned creature. My problem was alcohol, and I needed to do something about it.

I did — I stopped taking the first drink. Today I am alive in my life, alive in God's world and enjoying this universe.

When I think clearly, I know I belong.

*"A free society is one where it is safe to
be unpopular."*

Adlai Stevenson

Tough love requires that at times I must say
or do things that make me "unpopular". That
is part of the spiritual risk of loving: to be
popular is not always to be right!

As an alcoholic I was a people-pleaser;
concerned with saying what people wanted to
hear, do what people expected, remain silent
rather than cause upsets. I was afraid that if
I said what I really thought, I might be rejected.
My self-esteem was secondary to what other
people thought of me.

Today in my sobriety I love myself enough
to say what I believe and do what I consider
right. I refuse to remain silent when confronted
with injustice or the addictions of others. My
spiritual program risks the possibility of being
unpopular.

*Teach me to always say and do what I believe
to be true.*

"The saints are the sinners who keep on going."
                                    Robert Louis Stevenson

At times I do not want to carry on; I do not want to fight anymore for truth and freedom; it seems so much easier to "give up" and agree with everybody — but I know, deep inside myself, this is not true.

At times the disease speaks to me and tells me to "give up" and everything will be okay — perhaps have one drink, don't rush off to so many meetings, get what you can when you can! It all sounds so tempting, but I know that it does not work.

Sobriety works! The struggle and pain to act responsibly in my life is paying off and it does get better. I am not going to give up. My life is worth more than a quick fix!

Lord, let me know that true courage is working through the pain.

*"Humor may be defined as the kindly
contemplation of the incongruities of life and
the artistic impression thereof . . .
The essence of humor is human kindliness."*
Stephen Leacock

Humor for me is a key to balance. In the joke I am able to release some tension or frustration and cope with my disease of alcoholism. When I drank, I did not have a genuine sense of humor — rather it was sarcasm, cruel "put-downs" or insane expressions of my manic personality. My fun was created at the expense of others. It was a form of violence. It kept people away from me and created a loneliness in my life.

Today I seek to use humor as an expression of acceptance, tolerance, understanding and forgiveness. Humor is an aspect of my spiritual program. In humor I experience God.

*Give me the gift of humor that reflects the dignity
and hope for us all.*

"Sanity is madness put to good use."
George Santayana

I heard the phrase "make the disease work for you". It made a great deal of sense to me and still does. I am a recovering alcoholic. My alcoholism is still within me and every day I take the necessary steps to stay sober. My disease is that "mad" part of me that wants to destroy my life, relationships and understanding of God. What I need to do is accept my "madness" and turn it around so that it works for me. My suffering is the key to my spiritual growth. My anger and manipulation helps me to understand the imperfections of others. My powerlessness over alcohol gives me an understanding of humility that is based on reality. The acceptance of my "madness" keeps me sane!

O God, give me the sanity to accept my imperfections so that I can grow into the "best" that I can be.

"Science may have found a cure for most evils; but it has found no remedy for the worst of them all — the apathy of human beings."
                                        Helen Keller

I read today of a woman who ate herself to death. Friends and family when interviewed said, "She simply didn't seem to care." She had stuffed her feelings for so long that she had forgotten what they were; she had lost her spirituality. Apathy kills people.

So long as people do nothing, the disease of addiction gets worse and more victims are claimed. Apathy feeds ignorance because it stops activity; apathy stops life.

The antidote for apathy is spirituality. The spiritual person is alive with positive attitudes and creative hope — he is infectious. People are challenged to discover a meaning to life in their own lives. Hope produces recovery; recovery produces a message that must be shared; in the message is the miracle of life.

I pray that in the face of apathy I can discover hope.

*"I love my country better than my family; but I
love humanity better than my country."*
Francois Fenelon

We need to think "big". We need to escape
from those little concepts that keep us small.
Life is more than we can ever perceive. We
need to see it in its totality. The nuclear family
can be restrictive if taken as the center of our
loyalty. Even our national citizenship needs to
be placed in the context of the world. Our
freedom rests in our universal humanity.

Spirituality is about thinking "big". It is
finding God in the richness of His creation.
Our insistence on our shared humanity is the
path to world peace and serenity. Divisions
should not exist for the humanitarian who
seeks acceptance for all men simply because
they are men.

*May I seek to find the One in the many — and
the many in the One.*

"God will forgive me; that's his business."
                                    Heinrich Heine

It took me a long time to accept that God had forgiven the deeds done in my addiction. It took me a long time to comprehend that God is forgiveness, "forgiving love". Forgiveness unites us with God because it is His nature to forgive.

When I am living the spiritual life, I can unite myself with Him by my acts of forgiveness. And when I forgive others, I am doing a kindness, an act of forgiveness, to myself. Hate used to drain me of energy and it still can if I get caught up in resentments. Forgiveness restores energy and peace.

When I forgive, I am at one with God.

In the forgiveness of others I discover me.

*"No matter how old you get, if you keep the desire
to be creative, you're keeping the man-child alive."*
                                        John Cassavetes

When I was a child, I used to play in the
sand and make castles. I would build a strong
and firm fortress around the castle so that it
could withstand the force of the sea.

Today I also like to play in my life and I
need to build strong and firm behavioral
structures that will withstand pressure and
stress. Today I need to build my life on a sure
foundation — and that foundation must be me!
I need to take care of me so that I can enjoy
my life.

How do I take care of me? I watch what
I drink. I am a recovering alcoholic, and so I
choose not to drink alcohol. I drink soda,
orange juice and milk — but no alcohol. This
is an important part of my self-love program.
I exercise regularly. I watch what I eat and I
avoid sugar and needless carbohydrates. I rest
in the evenings and take walks in the fresh
air. The child that is in me still lives, but today
he is healthy.

*Help me to treat life responsibly, but not
too seriously.*

"Language is the light of the mind."
                    John Stuart Mill

When I was drinking, I never really thought about how I behaved, how I dressed or the language I used. Today I believe I should be responsible for the "whole" of me.

Language is important because it is my "bridge" to others; it is also the vehicle for understanding the ideas of others. Spirituality involves the concept of language because it is the means of growth, communication and relationship. My words help me to be known. My ability to understand the ideas and aspirations of others helps me to feel that I belong.

God is perceived in His world and the gift of language is one of the ways He makes Himself known. My words are spiritual.

May the light of God's eternal truth be manifested in the way I talk and relate to others.

*"I know of no more encouraging fact than the
unquestionable ability of man to elevate his life
by a conscious endeavor."*
                              Henry David Thoreau

Life is exciting to me when I am creating,
when I am pursuing a dream, when I am making
miracles in my life.

I suppose "perseverance" stems from a belief
that things get better when we roll-up our
sleeves and do something. Sobriety is about
comprehending that in our lives we reflect the
message.

God has created man with the ability to
make the dream come true; this is not to say
it is easy . . . but it is harder not to dream!

*Teach us to wonder at the stars with a spade in
our hands.*

> *"The art of teaching is the art of assisting discovery."*
>
> *Mark Van Doren*

I have a need of a "sponsor" in my life. Somebody I turn to when I have problems, when I am confused or in pain, when I simply need to talk, when I feel lonely or when I am about to make a major change in my life. Every addict needs a sponsor; somebody to bounce ideas off, especially ideas that affect the living of my life because I truly understand that the disease of alcoholism lives in my life!

My sponsor guides, suggests and gently leads me to where I need to go; he does not demand or dictate. My sponsor is a friend whom I can trust, and he makes a point of not being a "fixer" in my life. He will not allow me to escape into his life. He will not allow me to become addicted to him.

O God, let me always be free enough to discover You in my life.

*"It is all one to me if a man comes from Sing Sing
or Harvard. We hire a man not his history."*
                                        Henry Ford

So often we can get so locked into our
history — what we did, what we said, the
events of which we were ashamed — that we
miss the gift of the new day.

Those of us who suffer from the disease of
addiction need to deal with past problems but
not live in them. Our attitude towards today
need not be based on what happened yesterday.
Today is the beginning of the rest of our lives.
Today I know that I create most of the pain
and tragedy in my life, but I also know that
I create the joys and successes. I am confident
that today will be a success. I am confident
that my sobriety makes me a winner.

*Lord, I forgive myself for yesterday and look
forward to the healing that comes with today.*

*"The future is hidden even from the men who
made it."*

Anatole France

Life is a glorious mystery. We can never fully
understand it and it will always confuse and
amaze us. After we have understood one thing,
we are presented with a fresh problem. We are
not perfect. We are not God. We will never
understand completely.

Some years ago this used to anger and irritate
me. I wanted to know everything. I wanted to
have the answer to all life's problems. I wanted
the "power" that comes with perfection. I
hated being vulnerable, weak and confused! I
hated being human. Yes, that was my problem.
I hated being a human being.

Today I am enjoying the adventure of life,
and I kneel in awe at its mingled complexity.
Today life is a paradox that I can live with.

Help me to accept the mystery of life.

*"Opinions cannot survive if one has no chance to
fight for them."*

　　　　　　　　　　　　　　Thomas Mann

An opinion is worth fighting for, and I have
opinions on a great number of subjects — as
a result of sobriety.

Drugs have a tendency to make insane
remarks appear brilliant; the drunk is always
the unsung poet or victimized genius when he
is "in alcohol". I did not have opinions when
I was drinking but rather a series of chaotic
and incoherent reactions.

But today I have considered opinions. I am
able to think and make decisions. I am able
to make a contribution to life and the world
in which I live. I am involved.

More than this, today I have the spiritual
confidence to fight for what I believe and
"speak out" my concerns in love. Today I am
alive and I love it — also I love me.

*Let me always hear the opinions of others but not
fail to express my own.*

"For here we are not afraid to follow wherever it may lead, nor to tolerate error so long as reason is free to combat it."

Thomas Jefferson

As an alcoholic I was so often afraid to challenge the thinking and ideas of other people. My "people pleasing" demanded peace at any price. And yet so much of what I heard, read and practiced I did not agree with. Now I see that my behavior, my attitude — along with the alcohol consumption — kept me sick.

In my spiritual program today I am free to reject, consider and have my own opinions in life. I do not simply have to agree with everything that is said, in this way I am discovering my value and self-esteem.

Lord, I am grateful for the freedom to cooperate.

"All wars are civil wars, because all men are brothers . . . Each one owes infinitely more to the human race than to the particular country in which he was born."

Francois Fenelon

My disease of addiction kept me separate, isolated and alone. I was so busy seeing how I was different from other people that I missed the similarities. I missed the "oneness" of this creation by always placing myself above it, below it, outside it: and I was the loser.

Even my religion kept me separate. I was a Christian and not a Jew, Muslim or Hindu — but I failed to see the similarities of these major philosophies; I failed to see what all religious people have in common; I failed to see the inclusiveness of Love, Truth and Forgiveness.

God is to be found in the "difference" and "sameness" of His people.

O Lord, I am discovering that even the differences, when understood, become the same.

> *"I would I could stand on a busy corner, hat in*
> *hand, and beg people throw me their*
> *wasted hours."*
>
> *Bernard Berenson*

I enjoy my sobriety so much that I hate to waste my time. Part of my spiritual program involves a correct use of time. I will not spend time with negative or destructive people. I will not spend time in useless gossip or doing things I do not enjoy to please other people.

I am enjoying life so much I do not wish to waste any of it. Spirituality involves a creative stewardship of time.

As an alcoholic I wasted so much time. For most of my life I was "out to lunch"! Today I spend time enjoying my life — and I spend quality time alone with "self". I enjoy my little conversations with self — the thoughts I have and need to ponder upon. I need time to rest in the peace of my life. Time is a precious gift from God that should not be wasted.

Lord, let me live each day as if it were my last.

*"The real problem is in the hearts and minds
of men."*
Albert Einstein

We are facing not so much a "drug problem" as a "people problem" — and this requires a solution from the people. I believe the solution and recovery has already been given by God, but it must be discovered from within. We need to seek out what is truly in our minds and hearts: what are our problems, what are our needs, what do we long for, where are we going in our lives?

Today it is not enough for me to know my problems, I need also to talk about them. Today I choose to express my feelings.

*God, I thank You for the creative gift
of communication.*

"Men love to wonder, and that is the seed
of science."
                    Ralph Waldo Emerson

In my sobriety the world is a wonderful place.
I often sit back and am amazed at the splendor
of life, at the simple happenings that give such
joy, at the nobility that is revealed in man,
at the creative adventure and mystery of life.
I meditate in wonder.

Now I see how drugs kept me blind from
so much. Alcohol kept me a prisoner of
mediocrity and much of the wonder of life
passed me by. As a drinking alcoholic I existed
in life, rather than lived life. I was a bored
spectator rather than a participant. I reacted
to things, rather than initiated events. Alcoholism equals dullness. Recovery symbolizes
energy.

Today I can dream dreams and rest in the
wonder of it all. God is good.

O Lord, let me see the wonderful mystery of life
even in the ordinary.

"Beauty is not caused. It is."
> *Emily Dickinson*

So many people think that beauty is what you do to yourself; what you wear, makeup, clothes, hairstyles or expensive jewelry. Again it is so easy to get caught up in "things". Reality is not about what we wear but who we are.

The beauty that God has created comes from within. The twinkle in the eyes that says "hello". The hug that says "I love you". The gentle embrace and smile that says "I forgive you". The tear that cries "I understand".

When God said to the world, "It is good", Beauty was born. Drugs and crazy relationships only get in the way of us being what we were intended to be: beautiful for God.

Today I seek to put God's beauty in my actions, words and attitudes.

"No man is a failure who is enjoying life."
                              William Feather

Spirituality is fun. I enjoy my sobriety today and I do not take myself too seriously.

For years I thought I was a failure and this "thought" manifested the behavior of a failure. I hid, sulked, was jealous, carried resentments and isolated myself from life — and then blamed the world.

Today because I really understand and accept that I am a child of God, I know that I am not a failure and I have a glorious future in recovery. Today I have hope. Today I have confidence. Today I am able to accept and forgive. Today I am able to love my neighbor because I love myself.

In my enjoyment of life may I reflect your love for the world.

"Though pride is not a virtue, it is the parent of many virtues."
> *M. C. Collins*

I need to remember that "pride" is not necessarily a negative. It is sensible to have a balanced pride in my sobriety because self-esteem will grow from the pride and respect I give to myself. God has made me and is involved with me and, therefore, I am a beautiful person.

Balanced pride helps me with my appearance, grooming and personal etiquette that comes with clothes, fashion and hairstyles. Pride helps me with my communication skills — I work hard at being understood, speaking out clearly and developing better methods of being understood.

Pride stops me from being taken advantage of, enabling me to say "no" to others while still feeling good about myself. A healthy sense of pride is essential for spiritual growth.

Lord, let me have a realistic appreciation of myself that leads to achievement.

"You just wake up one morning and you got it!"
Moms Mabley

I am so busy living I don't think about "getting old". I am so grateful in my recovery from alcoholism that tomorrow, the future and age are secondary.

In my sickness I was always living in the future; what would tomorrow bring? Will I die crippled, lonely and afraid? My projections into the future produced an emotional pain.

Today I do not need to do this. I welcome old age because I bring into it the joy and experience of my sobriety. Will I be lonely? I doubt it if I stick to my recovery program; I have so many friends all over the world meeting together to face the disease on a daily basis. Also I know that nothing could ever compare with the loneliness of my drinking days.

My spiritual program reminds me to be grateful for my life and this includes the inevitability of old age.

Lord, as I grow in age may I also grow in wisdom and tolerance.

*"It takes a wise man to handle a lie; a fool had
better remain honest."*
Norman Douglas

As a drinking alcoholic I was telling so many
lies to cover the lies I had previously told that
I got lost in a maze of untruth! Most of the
lies were stupid, irrelevant and harmless — but
they were all aimed at building up my ego.
Making me look good. Telling people I had
more. My memory could not keep up with my
tongue and I became guilty, ashamed and
embarrassed.

Today I need to remember that there is
nothing any lie can give me that I need; there
is nothing in the world of fabrication that I
need; I have what I need.

Today I have a relationship with a God and
Friend that I can understand and be vulnerable
with; I don't need to be perfect to be loved.

*Help me to seek the good life in those things that
are good.*

*"No one is useless in this world who lightens the
burdens of another."*
                                    Charles Dickens

As a drunk I thought that the world owed
me a living. Everybody existed for my employment and service; the world was waiting for
my telephone call! For years I manipulated
people, and I was such a good "con" they often
left thanking me!

Today a part of my spiritual program requires
service. I make the coffee, put out the cookies,
cook the meal and invite friends for dinner.
I make the telephone call, give the lectures,
share in groups and write articles. The life of
service helps to keep me sober. I am the
message that I share. And I do it for me!

*Thank You for making me aware of my need
to give.*

"Real generosity towards the future consists in giving all to what is present."
                    Albert Camus

Much of the gratitude that I talk about needs to be centered in what I do with today: I need to focus on the present, rather than procrastinate for the future.

As a sick alcoholic I lived either in the guilt of yesterday or the fear of tomorrow — missing the reality of the present. The present moment is all that I have and through this "moment" I live and breathe and have my existence!

My understanding of prayer is centered in the present moment because any understanding of relationship and communication, especially with God, must begin from where one is, rather than where one would like to be. Spirituality is the reality of the moment.

Master, thank You for the life that is experienced in the moment.

"Nothing can bring you peace but the triumph of principles."
Ralph Waldo Emerson

Slowly I am understanding what principles are in my life. I am learning to live with a code of ethics that I do not always like, but I know is good for me and others. Although I do not always fully understand the "spiritual principles" of life, I know that my ongoing recovery should be based upon them.

Some of the "spiritual principles" by which I try to live are: Honesty, Truth, Openness, Forgiveness, Acceptance, Humility and Hope.

I am also experiencing a personal satisfaction in knowing that I am living today with a set of principles that work. They enable me to be a feeling and loving human being. Today I am beginning to feel what I always thought other people had. Today I am alive in my life.

May Your principles be my lifestyle.

"Every man, on the foundation of his own
   sufferings and joys, builds for all."
                                    Albert Camus

In my pain I am able to reach out to others. When I share my pain, I not only understand but I am understood. It is my pain and suffering that unites me with others. Other people become a part of my life and are involved in who I am.

Through my shared feelings, other people begin to share. Trust develops across this bridge of understanding. Feelings unite the world.

Lord, You created us in ONENESS — help us in
   our struggle to unite.

*"I tend to be suspicious of people whose love of
animals is exaggerated; they are often
frustrated in their relationship
with humans."*
Yila (Camilla Koffler)

Anything can be used to avoid dealing with
reality. People can use alcohol, food, drugs,
people, sex, gambling — and yes, even animals
— to avoid dealing with their loneliness and
feelings of isolation.

The key to addiction is to be found in the
obsessive and compulsive behavior patterns
that stop us from reaching our full potential
as human beings. We cannot relax with who
we are because of our exaggerated and painful
lifestyles. We cannot truly love ourselves
because of our obsession with the "it" that
seems to be controlling us. At some point we
need to see the obsession and begin to talk
about it.

In order for me to be a spiritual person I
must free myself from compulsive attitudes.

*God, I meditate on the "comfortableness"
of freedom.*

"May you live all the days of your life."
                                    Jonathan Swift

I heard a story that offers a key to the meaning of spirituality:

Two little fish were huddled together, afraid to move. A large fish swam by them, confident and strong. The big fish shouted out to the two little fish, "Why don't you swim out and enjoy the beautiful ocean?" The two little fish looked at each other and asked, "Where is the ocean?" They were in it but they didn't know it!

As an alcoholic I existed in life but I didn't live: I missed vacations, people, friendships, feelings, nature, sunsets and God. Like so many addicts, I was numbered amongst the "walking dead". Today I continue to make a spiritual choice that avoids alcohol and I am able to feel again. Today I am alive.

In You I live to love and love to live.

*"People who take time to be alone usually have
depth, originality and quiet reserve."*
                                                    John Miller

I need to be alone. I need time to listen to
my thoughts, consider my opinions and
strengthen my body. I need to pull away from
my hectic life to be alone with me.

As a drinking alcoholic I hated to be alone.
I became paranoic about "leaving the fort" —
today I accept that nobody is indispensable and
that the world will still be there when I return
from the desert!

Today I grow in the stillness of solitude. I
can rest in that "still" part of me that is the
essential me.

God is very close to me in the silence of
self.

*Lord, in the stillness of Your life, I am healed
and rejuvenated.*

> *"You grow up the day you have the first real*
> *laugh — at yourself."*
>   *Ethel Barrymore*

Today I can laugh at myself. I do not take myself too seriously and I am beginning to grow. I used to be so serious. Having the "poor me's", sitting on my pity pot demanding attention; I was so unhappy. And I was causing my unhappiness.

Then a friend listened to my complaints for half-an-hour and then began to laugh, giving out a real belly-laugh and at that point I began to laugh, too! My attitude was so stupid, selfish and futile that it demanded a laugh to shake me out of it — at that point I began to grow.

Today I laugh at my funny little ways, my funny little walk, my ridiculous pretensions, my grandiose behavior. Today with the laughter comes humility.

O Lord, let me experience the miracle of laughter.

"Power does not corrupt. Fear corrupts, perhaps
the fear of loss of power."
John Steinbeck

In my recovery I am beginning to understand that so much "power" in the world is really fear. The power that seeks to attack first in order to feel secure is really fear. The power that always has to have an answer is really fear. The power that arrogantly refuses to listen is really fear. So much power is "fear" dressed in illusion!

Spiritual power has the ability to be vulnerable. It can live with confusion. It can stand alone. It allows others to walk away to pursue their happiness. Spiritual power can exist in suffering and loneliness, and it does not expect perfection.

My recovery is teaching me to live and let others live, too. My freedom must respect the freedom of others; respect is a two-way street!

Give me the power that can rest in imperfection.

"Any God I ever felt in Church I brought in with me. And I think all the other folks did, too. They come to Church to share God, not find God."
                                                      Alice Walker

God is within us! At one time I would find that statement blasphemous or incomprehensible. I always thought God was a long way off — separate, unknowable and judgmental. He was much more a judge than a friend. I saw myself more the sinner than the son. Naturally, with such a low self-esteem it was hard to associate God with my life, let alone consider God existing within me!

Then I began to search for the spiritual path that leads to a deeper understanding of self — and I found a loving, gentle and friendly God. His love was so pervasive in His world that I was able to discover Him in my life and the lives of others. The concept of meeting together to share God made sense. The concept of discovering a God within and without made God knowable and comprehensible. Because God lives in me, I am alive.

Master, in the breaking of the bread, may I share Your life in my world.

*"Freedom is the right to choose: the right to create
for yourself the alternatives of choice. Without the
possibility of choice and the exercise of choice a
man is not a man but a member, an instrument,
a thing. . ."*
Archibald MacLeish

Spirituality involves the freedom to change;
it requires the variety of choice in order to
grow.

My past addiction was a life of slavery
because it removed from me creative choice
and left me obsessing about drugs and alcohol.
My life, conversation and thoughts revolved
around the bottle, and I was oblivious to the
true meaning of life. I could not "do better"
in my life because I was addicted not only to
drugs but to the destructive lifestyle that goes
with them. My freedom to experience the
spiritual power of God's creativity was lost to
a mindless craving for drugs; in this sense, drug
addiction is slavery.

Today I am free to see God's world in people,
places and things and I make a choice to live,
love and laugh.

*I am growing in the awareness of
Your multifaceted love for me.*

"There is nothing permanent except change."
                                        Heraclitus

Today I know that I need to change. I accept that my behavior and attitude was negative and destructive. Today I make a choice to work on my addiction. I was changing before I embraced a spiritual program but the change was for the worse. Each day I grew more dependent, more isolated, more angry and depressed. I felt I was a hopeless case!

Today I am working on my anger and loneliness. I talk about those things that cause me pain and distress. I express my fears and resentments — and it is getting better.

God created this world in perpetual change and I believe that He is to be discovered in the change. I am evolving into Truth with my small steps towards recovery. The steps I take towards recovery are my "yes" to God.

In the daily changes I discover the stability of God.

*"A man who dares to waste one hour of time has
not discovered the value of life."*
                                          Charles Darwin

Life is not to be wasted. Time is not to be
wasted. Friends, relationships, opportunities are
not to be wasted. Why? Because as vulnerable
human beings we do not have the ultimate
control of our lives and none of us know when
our lives will end, when we shall die, when time
and opportunity will be no more! Life is too
precious to waste.

During my years as an addict I did not value
my life. I did not value time. I did not value
friends and relationships. Nothing was valued
except the alcohol! Life was meaningless. God
was absent and I felt nothing — just a "dullness" at the center of my being. Today this
is not the case. Through my pain I have found
the value of life and I have discovered a God
as I understand Him.

God, let me value what I have while I have it.

> *"I have my own particular sorrows, loves,*
> *delights; and you have yours. But sorrows,*
> *gladness, yearning, hope, love belong to all of us,*
> *in all times and in all places. Music is the*
> *only means whereby we feel these emotions in*
> *their universality."*
>
> H. A. Overstreet

A language for the world is music. It unites all peoples, cultures, religions and backgrounds; it points man beyond himself, while at the same time breathing through him God's glory. Music makes man wonder, enables him to dream, allows him to rest in the miracle of creativity.

Drugs stopped me from appreciating the gift of music. They twisted and corrupted sounds and made them destructive and coarse. Drugs took from me so much and left me with a feeling of utter emptiness.

In my recovery I can hear again. My spiritual program incorporates music, different types of music, the inexhaustible joys of melody. I can feel in it, through it, with it — another miracle.

Thank You for the gift of music that enables me to
grow in my understanding of self and my need
of others.

"To say that a man is made up of certain chemical elements is a satisfactory description only for those who intend to use him as a fertilizer."
Herbert J. Muller

Man is more than chemicals. Man is more than an animal. Man is a human being, carrying the image of God, the imprint of Divinity, the power of the creative God.

As an addict I doubted myself, only adding to my "powerlessness" and "unmanageability". I internally said, "I can't" before I tried. My low self-esteem was evident long before I took a drink. I was always trying to get my "outsides" to match what I imagined your "insides" to be like.

When I accepted my alcoholism I was able to discover God in my life. Today I am able to create through Him and in Him. Spirituality comes with the awareness of our God-given divinity.

May I never cease to see You in my life.

"Man is what he believes."
                              Anton Chekhov

My miracle is that I now believe in me.
Today I accept my disease of addiction and I
do not resist or deny it. I believe that I am
an alcoholic. I believe that I am an overeater.
I am a co-dependent. I believe that I am an
adult child of an alcoholic. And this belief
enables me to be free.

For too long I played the game of control;
blaming and bargaining — and I lost. Now I
choose to surrender to the reality of who I am.
I accept my disease on a daily basis and I make
choices with the awareness of my disease. And
it is getting better.

My belief about my addiction has also given
me an insight into God and His gift of freedom.
He loves me enough to give me choice and
with this gift comes responsibility. I believe that
I am responsible for how I live with my
addictions. Today I accept that responsibility.

What I believe reflects the God I believe in;
I believe in Freedom.

"In the country of the blind the one eyed king can still goof up."

Anonymous

For years I tried to control everything and everybody. Things had their place; there was a correct code of behavior for doing things; everything had to have its place. I felt responsible for the universe and everybody in it.

Today I can laugh at my mistakes and the mistakes of others. When I catch myself organizing the world, I remember where the "perfect" yesterdays got me — and I laugh. God made me with a navel and flat feet; I would have preferred something different but there is a loving message within my imperfections. It is okay to goof up!

Today I relax in the humor of being human.
Thank You for making me an angel in the dirt.

"If the work of God could be comprehended by reason, it would be no longer wonderful, and faith would have no merit if reason provided proof."
                                        Pope Gregory I

Some things happen that I do not understand or comprehend, but I have faith that they will happen tomorrow: sunsets, night following day, the song of the bird, the colors of nature, and the joy and adventure of being alive. Perhaps the biggest mystery for mankind to grapple with is love — a man will suffer, endure persecution, even be put to death for that which he loves; the pain and sorrow of love is mingled into what it is to be a human being.

Reason does not have the answer to life. Faith is the medication for our existence. We have a belief in tomorrow because of what we have experienced today. If I can say "no" to alcohol today then I can do it tomorrow — if I really want to.

Lord, let me not seek for proof but daily seek to grapple with the problems of life.

*"All religions must be tolerated . . .
for . . . every man must get to heaven
his own way."*
                    Frederick the Great

There are many ways to God and I believe that Christianity is one way. However, I am convinced that there are other ways with or without religion. My experience of the church has been good, and I have been encouraged to question and doubt, search for new areas of faith within my agnosticism, explore other religions. My experience of Christianity has been supportive of openness and compassion.

God is not a prisoner of any religion and we can all learn from each other's experiences — but we need to listen. To dismiss arrogantly the value that a religion can bring is, to my way of thinking, as negative and sick as to accept what a religion says without question.

*Let me find in the religions of the world the
ONENESS of Your truth.*

"It is never too late to give up your prejudices."
                              Henry David Thoreau

Prejudice divides people and feeds upon anger, resentment and fear. Today I can see that my prejudices stemmed from my seeing in others what I disliked in myself. I hated people who appeared "weak" because I knew that I was weak and vulnerable. I hated people who were "different" because I knew there were parts of me that were different from how I appeared. I hated the people who stood up for their principles and talked about their feelings because, as a drunk, I never really had any principles and I couldn't get in touch with my feelings.

Today I try to talk about my prejudices and overcome them. A knowledge of those people I disliked has proven useful in slowly overcoming my prejudices.

Teach me to locate myself in my criticism
of others.

*"Man, unlike the animals, has never learned that
the sole purpose of life is to enjoy it."*
                                        Samuel Butler

Spirituality enables me to enjoy my life. I enjoy my sobriety. I enjoy the freedom of a "God as I understand Him". I enjoy the fellowship of ideas and opinions that are based on love and honest sharing. The world is to be enjoyed and not endured! God is fun.

For years I thought that God was a judge to be feared; angry, hostile and revengeful. Strange how silly this all seems now, but for years I was afraid of God and feared His presence. Then I was introduced to a God who is beyond institutions and dogmas, free of creeds and punishments, a loving and joyous God who created me to be happy. Today I am enjoying my freedom.

*God, the Father of the Universe, is also "Daddy"
to us all.*

"Originality does not consist in saying what no one has ever said before, but in saying exactly what you think yourself."

James Stephens

Sometimes I surprise myself with what I say, think or contemplate. Within my being is a very strange world that I wish to share with others. Why? Because if I am truly honest about what I think and feel, it may unite me with the true identity of others. Perhaps we are all a little strange! However I will never know what people are thinking or feeling unless I take a risk and share my honest feelings. My involvement with my fellow man revolves around my honesty.

In the knowledge of Your love let me share my feelings.

No man is a
failure
who is enjoying
life.

William Feather

*"Nobody ever outgrows Scriptures; the book
widens and deepens with our years."*
          Charles Haddan Spurgeon

Not so long ago I had a narrow and rigid
religious outlook that was based solely on my
narrow belief system. I was addicted to my
religious approach and any alternative or
variation was condemned before investigation.
I was a religious bigot. I was a hypocrite. I hid
behind my dogma and practiced ritual.

Today I have a comprehensive view of
religion and God, thanks to the influence of
recovering alcoholics and the discovery of a
spiritual program. Today I am able to see the
depth and richness of scripture, a living library
of books and experiences. Today I am able to
see beyond the printed word to the message
of healing and love that comes with honesty
and acceptance. Now I know that the bigoted
side of me was fearful and afraid of change.
I needed rules to keep people from discovering
what a lonely and spiritually bereft person I
was. The rules and dogmas formed my prison
bars. I was drowning in religiosity. Today I am
free to be different. Today I am free to be me.

*O wind of Truth, continue to blow and inspire us
through our differences.*

*"Facts do not cease to exist because they
are ignored."*
                                        Aldous Huxley

Reality is not dependent upon our acceptance. Addiction does not have to be accepted
to be real. Alcoholism was killing people long
before it had a name!

I need to remember this in the recovery
program for my life. A big part of my life was
spent denying that I had a problem. My
manipulative art was exercised in discovering
more acceptable excuses for my drunkenness,
rather than looking at the problem. I danced
towards death with God and denial on my lips.
Belief in the God of Truth did not stop my
dishonesty.

The process of self-love and acceptance
began in my cry for help. Surrender brought
me sanity. God was working His purpose out
in my life because I was getting out of my way;
I was facing the facts. Spirituality is making the
words fit the feelings, and the feelings make
the action.

Help me never to ignore what I know to be true.

"God sees nothing average."
                                    Anonymous

God created every human being from the dust and yet He bestowed within all of us His image. This means that we are divine. We are creatures created to create. We share God's life for the universe. We are anything but average!

And yet for years we thought we were not good enough. We needed drugs, food or people to make us okay. We considered ourselves "less-than", inferior or freaks.

But today we awake to a new message. The spiritual message tells us that we are forever holding the hand of God. He needs you and me to work in His vineyard. In us He makes miracles. Today I know that I am beautiful. I am important. I am unique.

Master, part of Your beauty is in Your healing power. Help me to be healed daily by beholding my beauty that is forever within and without.

"War is only a cowardly escape from the problems of peace."

Thomas Mann

Sometimes it is easier to attack than it is to discuss and seek harmony. It is easier to lash out, hurt, maim or destroy than it is to listen, forgive, understand and reconcile. Violence is so often the cowardly way out.

The sadness for our society is that war and violence are often presented as manly or heroic. Our modern heroes so often carry weapons rather than the olive branch. Surrender is seen as cowardice. Gentleness is seen as weakness. The diplomat is seen as the schemer.

My recovery teaches me that nothing is gained by acts of violence, whereas in the atmosphere of peace, God and man can be reconciled.

Give me the courage to surrender on a daily basis and bring harmony into my world.

*"Hope is the pillar that holds up the world. Hope
is the dream of the working man."*
                                    Pliny the Elder

I look at the world and I discover an order,
a pattern to life, a balance within the system.
I do not believe in a God of chaos. I find a
spiritual stability in creation. Night follows day;
people, regardless of culture or creed, are
remarkably similar in feelings and needs; death
makes way for life. The God who created this
world has given the seeds of hope within the
living of life. I am the key to the understanding
of the universe.

In this observation I find hope. If I continue
to go with the flow of life, I will find peace
and stability. It is only when I fight the system
that I experience pain.

*May the God of order and stability continue to
bring balance into my life by the spiritual changes
I continue to make.*

*"In every real man a child is hidden that wants
to play."*
                                        Friedrich Nietzsche

My spiritual program means that I can play
and have fun in my life. I am forty years old
and I can still enjoy going on the swings in
the park. But more importantly I have a daily
sense of adventure. My eyes light up as I ask:
How? When? Where? These words still dom-
inate my life.

I can still get excited about life; I can still
get excited about my life.

God is forever present in His world of color,
movement and change. But for me God is most
clearly seen in people. They are a constant
fascination for me. Part of my play involves
people-watching and as I gaze my mouth still
opens in amazement. The child in me still
enjoys the world in which I play.

*Thank You for toys, people and "difference" be-
cause they add color to my life.*

"There is no failure except in no longer trying."
Elbert Hubbard

I produced the failure in my life. For years I would blame everything and everyone — my parents, the job, my health, low income, a cruel world, thoughtless friends, the weather! Today I am able to own my failures because they are mine.

Today I am also able to see my successes — and this makes me a winner. I am able to see the things that I have achieved, the character defects I have confronted, the happiness that comes with an acceptance of self.

I may not be perfect but I am certainly not worthless. I may make mistakes but I am not evil. I have a heart that needs to love and also needs to be loved. Today I am able to reveal my vulnerability and discover its strength.

This underling is learning how to fly.

Master, may I continue to seek Your power and glory in my life.

"Where is there dignity unless there is honesty?"
                                        Marcus Cicero

The cornerstone of my life today is honesty. It is the quality I most desire in my life because I believe that with honesty comes a knowledge of God, self and relationships. It is the key to my recovery from addiction. It is the key to the meaning of spirituality. Honesty affords me hope for tomorrow.

As an alcoholic I was a dishonest man. I was not just dishonest because I told lies and manipulated the truth, I was dishonest because I refused to risk the journey into self. My dishonesty was not about what I said but what I did not say! Not so much about what I did but what I did not do. My dishonesty stopped me from discovering my God-given dignity.

Today I risk the journey into self and I am discovering more about God "as I understand Him". My level of honesty helps me to be happy and relaxed with who I am today.

"Be still and know that I am God." In the silence of self-honesty may I know myself.

"Poetry is the rhythmical creation of beauty
in words."

Edgar Allan Poe

Language helps us to understand and communicate. Poetry adds the dimension of "shape" and "movement". Poetry seems to go beyond words and ideas to the very essence of what life is about; it hints at divinity!

When I was drinking, I never understood the art of poetry. Today I use poetry as part of my adventure into meaning and self-knowledge.

So much more is open to me in sobriety, and I am able to appreciate things I never used to comprehend. Poetry is part of "it gets better".

Help me to seek You through all aspects of art.

"When one is painting, one does not think."
                    Raphael Sanzio

An artist is predominantly a person who feels rather than thinks; he is molding his most inner experiences into the finished product.

I am doing the same in my sobriety. Today I am molding something good and wholesome from a life that was negative and destructive. I am rediscovering God, not just in thoughts and ideas, but in the daily happenings of my life. God is not only an idea but He is alive in my relationships, behavior and daily acts of kindness.

God is a process in which I am involved. He is at the center of my life, regardless of the ordinariness of the event. Art is part of my life because I am a creative human being.

Teach me to look beyond the painting into myself.

> *"Procrastination — the art of keeping up with yesterday."*
>
> Don Marquis

Today I try to do all that I have set myself to do in a given day. I make a list of things that I need to do and a list of those things that I want to do — the things I "need" to do usually take priority.

This was not always the case. As a drinking alcoholic my life was littered with promises that were never kept, intentions that were never honored, appointments and meetings that did not happen. I pushed everything into tomorrow — and tomorrow never came.

My understanding of spirituality involves a responsibility for those things that I need to do. When I awake, I thank God for my sleep and I make a silent intention not to drink today; then I face my responsibilities. I separate my "needs" from my "wants" and I remember that I have a responsibility to other people: family, friends and colleagues. Today I am learning to live in my day.

Lord, may I do the things I should do and may I find time for those things I want to do.

"Man must cease attributing his problems to his environment and learn again to exercise his will, his personal responsibility in the realm of faith and morals."
Albert Schweitzer

God has created me to be a responsible human being and that means that I must seriously consider the choices and decisions that could affect my life and the lives of others. Today I understand that true freedom can only be experienced within the restraints of a responsible life.

For years I blamed other people for my drunken behavior — family, bishops, job, world situations — even God! But the truth was that I lived an irresponsible life around alcohol. I ignored the facts that surrounded my drinking.

Today I make a responsible decision not to drink, and I also take responsibility for my life. I cannot blame other people for the mistakes that I made. My real freedom is experienced in my responsibility.

Give me the freedom to impose my own constraints.

"Argument is the worst sort of conversation."
                                        Jonathan Swift

Why did I argue so much? Why *do* I argue so much! Usually it is because I feel threatened, angry, discounted or I am wrong and I do not want to admit it.

Today I need to remember that discussion is the better path to follow. I need to hear and understand what the other person is saying and from where they are coming. For too long I have argued, fought and produced enemies — today I wish to embrace the spiritual path of serenity and reconciliation. Also, I do not want to hurt anymore. Arguments hurt me. Arguments hurt others. I shout, push and scream but inside, afterwards, I hurt. My program today allows my ego to be balanced and restrained. I try to think before I speak. I consider before I react. However, when I do get into arguments and say hurtful and painful things that I do not mean, I am brave enough to say I am sorry.

May the God of peace, love and acceptance be seen in my relationships.

"A little theory makes sex more interesting, more
comprehensive and less scary. Too much is a
put-down, especially as you're
likely to get it out of perspective and become
a spectator of your own performance."
                                    Dr. Alex Comfort

We make too much of sex because we are
afraid of it. We abuse God's gift of sex by
placing it out of context, removing it from the
other things that make it meaningful, e.g.,
gentleness, trust, sensitivity, communication
and commitment.

The performance becomes more important
than the expression. The meaning gets lost in
the event. God's precious gift of sex is abused
by the sex act itself and it then begins to feed
on itself. Compulsive sex is only demonstrated
loneliness!

Spirituality teaches me to see all things as
part of God's gift of "wholeness" and sex is
an important part of this — but only a part.

God, in the awareness of my sexuality,
may I discover a relationship with myself,
others and You.

> *"To teach is to learn."*
> *Japanese Proverb*

The more I learn the more I know that I do not understand. Life is full of new and wonderful information; paradoxes and confusion abound; every new idea leads to a further truth — and the journey seems endless.

In a sense we are all disciples; we are all learning from each other and the role of teacher and student is forever being exchanged. In my sobriety I am able to see how many wonderful "things" exist in the world — so many fascinating and interesting places to visit, so many loving and insightful people. God has given me so much. I am so grateful to be able to learn in His garden.

Teacher, may I never stop learning and being a student in Your world.

*"Liberty means responsibility. That is why most
men dread it."*
                                        George Bernard Shaw

The fellowship of recovering addicts and
their families rejoice in the freedom of life; the
exchange of slavery to a drug or person for
liberty; a life of choice, rather than meaningless
compulsion.

But with the gift of liberty comes the weight
of responsibility. Today I am responsible for my
life. No longer can I say I do not know; no
longer can I blame others for my disease; no
longer can I manipulate in the "playground of
denial".

The spiritual program requires a maturity of
lifestyle that involves responsibility — but the
joys are immense.

*O Master of liberty and responsibility, let me not
forget to laugh.*

*"Tolerance is the positive and cordial effort to
understand another's beliefs,
practices and habits without
necessarily sharing or accepting them."*
                              Joshua Liebman

Today I am able to tolerate people, listen
to what they are saying and if I do not agree
with them, it is okay! I do not have to agree
with a person to tolerate or befriend him.

This is a new attitude for me and is part
of my spiritual program. When I was drinking,
I would not listen to people who had ideas
different to mine. I would not tolerate people
who had a different philosophy on life. Other
religions were discounted as being cultish,
crude or superstitious. I have learned that my
disease of alcoholism made me very arrogant
and narrow in my attitude to life — I rejected
two-thirds of the world as being heretical!

Today I can tolerate and learn from people
who view God, the world and morality differently from me. Spirituality is teaching me to
be open and accepting.

*Lord, may I find traces of Your love in different
philosophies and religions.*

"Faith has need of the whole truth."
                    Pierre Teilhard de Chardin

Faith is a journey that ends in God. Our understanding of imperfection teaches us to look beyond ourselves into the truth that is yet to be revealed. Our daily attitude adjustments bring us, step by step, to that truth and freedom that awaits us in the future.

Sufficient today to know that we are not God and nobody has all the answers. The hardest part of being a human being is accepting the limitations of our lives. Things happen without our involvement. We need not be there for existence to happen; there is life beyond me! God holds the world together, not me. Truth is in me but also beyond me. In this sense my faith is enriched by others, and at some point in the future we will all become ONE in truth.

*As I look to the future I see the Oneness
of tomorrow.*

*"Money is the symbol of duty. It is the sacrament
of having done for mankind that which mankind
wanted."*
                                        Samuel Butler

St. Paul said, "The laborer is worthy of his
hire." In one sense money — how people pay
us for the services we have performed — is
symbolic of our value in the community. Of
course, this is not always true and people can
make money by dishonest and destructive
methods.

However, in our society money is also a force
behind much creativity and job satisfaction.
The danger is to become a "snob". Thinking
that we are better than others because we earn
more money.

Spirituality is about discovering the "oneness" of mankind and incorporating our
creative "difference" — we can all learn from
each other. Pretentiousness is indicative of
insecurities that need to be dealt with in our
recovery program.

*O Lord, let my gratitude be seen in my relation-
ship with others.*

"You have not converted a man because you have silenced him."

Viscount John Morley

I need to remember that you cannot force a person into faith. You cannot make a person believe. You cannot bribe a person into prayer. So much of my early religion was "a deal": you do this and you will get this. If you do this for God and His church you will be happy and successful. There always seemed to be a "pay-off" with God, or that was how it seemed.

I think many of the silent majority sense the same kind of thing; God has got lost in "the business" of religion. Spirituality accepts the pain, confusion and anger of this silent majority and says, "find a God as you understand Him." Discover your power in your life — and then God will be perceived.

Lord, in my silence is the "shout" heard.

"Art flourishes where there is a sense of adventure."

                         A. N. Whitehead

Today I enjoy and am sustained by the adventure of life. The adventure of living. The adventure of living my life. For years I spent my time avoiding situations, avoiding people, avoiding me. Now in my daily recovery I need to participate and experience my spiritual energy. I want to meet new people. I want to travel. I want to work productively and earn money. I want to add something to this beautiful world.

I am discovering in my recovery that experiencing my creative spirituality makes me an artist. God is found in the hugs I give and the early morning "hellos" I shout to strangers. Today I am not afraid anymore. Today I am alive.

God, may I seek and find You in the small and mundane things of life; let me find You where I am.

"This could be such a beautiful world."
                                    Rosalind Welcher

The beauty that I see in the world also reveals a sadness — a sadness in knowing that it could be a much more loving and accepting place for everybody. If only we would "get together" in our difference instead of demanding "sameness".

We destroy so much God-given beauty by our desire to control, understand and arrogantly pursue a philosophy of selfishness — and we all lose.

But my spiritual hope for tomorrow comes in the creative choices I make today.

Let me be a good steward in Your world because it is Your gift to me.

*"Do what you can, with what you have, where
you are."*
                                    Theodore Roosevelt

Because we are not perfect, we need only
do our best. Because our recovery from addiction is an on-going process, we will discover
that our best is improving on a daily basis. It
is so easy to beat ourselves up emotionally by
thinking that our best is not good enough. Even
after years of recovery we still hear the old
tapes: "People do not want to listen to you."
"Is that all that you can do?"

We need to remember that the disease of
addiction still lives in our recovery. However,
our honest attempts at dealing with a problem
or helping another with a problem — provided
they are honest attempts — will usually be
more than sufficient.

Today I accept my best attempts with
gratitude and I am not too proud to seek the
advice of another.

*God, accept the best that I can offer as an
instrument of Your peace.*

*"My mother loved children — she would have
given anything if I had been one."*
Groucho Marx

For too many years I allowed myself to be
treated as a child. I played the child role in
order to avoid responsibility. Part of my people-
pleasing was living as a thirty-year-old child!
I was afraid to say "no". Afraid to disappoint
or hurt another's feelings. Afraid to tell my
parents how they were hurting me by their
need to control my life. God, when I think
about it, I spent years feeling guilty and afraid.

Today I am willing to deal with this pain
in my life; today I am willing to talk about it.
My biggest relief comes in knowing that I am
not alone. There are millions of us out there.
The difference is I have a program today that
enables me to talk about it.

*God, help me to be child-like without being child-
ish. Help me to grow into maturity
with a smile.*

"The growth of the human mind is still high adventure, in many ways the highest adventure on earth."

Norman Cousins

Today my life is an adventure. I am prepared for the unusual; I expect the confusion of life; I revel in God's reflected difference within creation: variety and the acceptance of variety is part of my joy in living.

God is to be found in the "odd" things in life: the dance, relationships, Charlie Chaplin, jogging, the pet dog and the sincere hug. The adventure we find in life reflects our adventure in God.

Spirituality is seeing beyond the ordinary into the extraordinary: "The Kingdom of God is within".

May I always seek to find You in the smallest and strangest of places.

*"That's one small step for man, one giant leap
for mankind."*
                                Neil A. Armstrong

Man is able to do such wonderful things in
this world. There is no end to what man can
achieve when he behaves responsibly and
honestly, working together with others to
discover more about himself and the universe.
God has truly made man in His own image
with all the power and creativity that that
implies.

The danger that forever surrounds man is
greed, pride and the misuse of "power".

As a recovering alcoholic I understand this
only too well. I wanted to control the situation
and keep other people out. I wanted to be the
best, I wanted to be out in front, and ego made
me arrogant and selfish. If this is true for me
and other human beings, it is also true for
governments, countries and alliances. Countries don't make wars, people do; countries
don't have achievements, people do — and this
universe must be seen as belonging to everyone
or it will belong to no one!

*Let us learn to enjoy and share Your garden and
not destroy it.*

*"Lord, grant that I may always desire more than I
can accomplish."*

Michelangelo

I must always "think big", not in an egotistical sense but as an adventure in spirituality.
When I had a small God, I always remained
a small person, with small aspirations and
dreams. Today I have an all-embracing inclusive God that fills the universe. Today I have
hope in my dreams.

As an alcoholic I missed so much. I observed
very little about myself and God's world, people
and friends became inconsequential; nothing
really mattered except the desire to drink. My
spiritual potential was lost in my alcoholism.

Today I am realizing my potential and I can
risk in sobriety. My motto has become "go for
it". Behind my dreams is my growth. I have
a sense of so much joy in the world that I wish
to enthusiastically experience my life.

God, I am so grateful to be alive.

*"He who begins by loving Christianity better than
Truth will proceed by loving his sect or church
better than Christianity, and end in loving
himself better than all."*
         Samuel Taylor Coleridge

My program for recovery from addiction is
spiritual and not religious. I believe that
spirituality encompasses all that is good and
noble in all the great religions of the world.
It cannot be confined or limited to one religion
or denomination. Spirituality is concerned for
truth wherever it may be revealed.

Spirituality stops the recovering person from
looking for the differences; it stops the arrogance and prejudice; it stops the division and
separations that feed the disease. Spirituality
emphasizes the inherent unity of man. It
teaches the most stubborn of men to hold
hands.

God the Creator is revealed in the variety
of His universe. I can find Him in the sunset,
the variety of animals, the love and care of
family and friends, the excitement and vision
of poetry and art, the inspiration of music.
Spirituality is . . . !

*Kneeling before the beauty of Your creation I
whisper "Amen".*

"The fault, dear Brutus, is not in the stars, but in ourselves that we are underlings."
                        William Shakespeare

My addiction to alcohol led me away from "self": today in my sobriety I am beginning to understand me. For years I blamed others for my misfortunes but today I see that I was the enemy in my life. It was a "cop-out" to blame God, family, job or life for my alcoholism — I needed to take responsibility for "self".

Part of my recovery program today involves me not looking "outside" for answers but looking within. The answer is not in the stars, not in fate — but rather in the destiny I create by the decisions I make today. I, and I alone, forge my future.

O Lord, let me create a life that is pleasing in Your sight.

*"We need to make a world in which fewer
children are born, and in which we take better
care of them."*
                                        Dr. George Wald

Spirituality is concerned for the physical.
How we plant seeds, do exercises and develop
a healthy food plan is as important as prayer,
reading and meditation. The body is part of
the soul.

Also we have a responsibility for the future;
for those who follow us on this planet. The
ecological welfare of our world is spiritual. An
irresponsibility concerning childbirth reveals an
arrogance that does not belong to the spiritual
program. The satisfaction of our personal
desires should never hurt the lives of others
— including the unborn.

*Teach me to have a spiritual responsibility
to the future.*

> *"Show me a thoroughly satisfied man — and I*
> *will show you a failure."*
>   *Thomas Alva Edison*

I need to strive for new things in my life.
I need to push out into new areas and discover
the richness of God's world. I need to explore
the varied creativity of creation.

There is so much that I have not done
because of the wasted years of my addiction.
So much that I have not seen, countries that
I have not visited, languages that I have not
learned and experiences that I have missed. My
compulsive and obsessive behavior left me a
prisoner of self — and also a victim of self.

The spiritual recovery I enjoy today says it
is okay for me to have things, enjoy things and
do things.

Help me to realize the energy and ambition You
have created within me.

"Old age is when you realize other people's faults are no worse than your own."

Edgar Shoaff

Age is a great leveler! I am on a journey to God and this involves many stages of experience — some good and some bad, some painful and some exceedingly joyful, some confusing and others understandable. These experiences will take me into a period of life called "old age".

Many people fear this period of life because it is connected with poor health, helplessness and death. I was afraid of age because a part of me feared the "mystery" of death. The "uncertainty" of death brought with it a lack of control! I am sure that guilt and a fear of God were also involved.

Today I realize that we all have similar fears and concerns. Mystery brings with it a sense of awe! Today I have a loving God. Today God is involved in my life. Today, in my recovery, I have a perspective in my life — I am not all bad! Age is bringing balance.

Thank You for the balance that comes with personal forgiveness.

*"Everything one does enough of eventually
generates its own interest and one then
begins to believe in it."*

Alan Dunn

I never thought that I could stay sober. For
years I tried to abstain with no success. It was
not the act of stopping that was different (I
could stop three times in one week!). It was
staying stopped.

Then a man said, "Try stopping for twenty-
four hours. If that proves too long, try stopping
until the morning or for one hour or even for
one minute . . . If the craving gets too severe,
call me but don't take that first drink!" My
abstinence began in periods of twenty-four
hours. Life is made up of days and we live in
periods of twenty-four hours, so I live a day
at a time. I was successful. I am successful.
Today I have a number of years that are based
on the simplicity of "don't drink today". I
believe in it. I believe in me. And it gets better.

*Lord of time, thank you for giving me the
simplicity of days, hours and minutes.*

*"I like the dreams of the future better than the
history of the past."*
                                Thomas Jefferson

I am an optimist. I believe that things are
getting better day by day. Today I believe that
what happened yesterday need not happen
today or tomorrow. Dreams can come true. I
know this to be true. Today I have dreams.
Today I have a hope for my life and on a daily
basis it is coming true. My life is becoming more
meaningful. Today my dreams have coincided
with God's dream for me.

Now I love myself enough to speak out for
me — and it feels good. Now my decision to
embrace the spiritual life is not dependent
upon others. Today I can dream to be me.

*Help me to dream with my feet firmly on
the ground.*

*"What is a man to profit if he shall gain the
whole world and lose his own soul?"*
Jesus (Mt. 16:26)

Spirituality brings with it a sense of priority
in my life: first things first. Unless I discover
me and have a love and respect for me, I have
nothing to offer in this world. I am the center
of my universe and through my life God is
radiated. I am a part of God's creative plan
and the pleasures of this world must be seen
as secondary to my developing a right relationship with God.

My disease of obsession and compulsion
wants me to place other things at the center
of my life: food, alcohol, drugs, people, money,
success, achievement and ego.

My spiritual program reminds me that my
love of self is shown in my refusal of the first
drink. If I am healthy, I can have the world;
without me, I can have nothing!

Let me find Your Kingdom that is within.

*"I do not feel obliged to believe that the same God
who has endowed us with sense, reason and
intellect has intended us to
forego their use."*
                                    Galileo Galilei

An essential part of being human is the ability to think, reflect and reason. Spirituality is involved in our ideas and perceptions because that is historically how man has grown and been able to change. As Descarte said, "Cogito ergo sum — I think therefore I am."

The tragedy is that few people experience the freedom to think and create because of the stifling addictions that are epidemic in our society: food, alcohol, drugs, religion, work, money and sex. We are so afraid of what others might think or say that we never fully experience our spiritual selves and everybody suffers. It is the "risks" in life that make man great.

*Help me to challenge what I do not believe in order
to discover what I do believe.*

*"As long as men are free to ask what they must
— free to say what they think — free to think
what they will — freedom can never be lost and
science can never regress."*
                                    J. Robert Oppenheimer

We need to press on in this wonderful
journey of life because new discoveries await
us in our tomorrows. Spirituality always brings
joy in the journey. In the traveling is the fun
for we will never reach our destination in this
life.

The freedom to question is the discipline of
science, and science is involved in the treatment and recovery of addiction. We must
always be looking for better ways of treatment,
more vivid ways of teaching and creative aids
to recovery.

Science, and every other creative discipline,
should be used in the treatment of addictions:
God is to be found in the many.

*Lord, let us remember that You gave mankind a
scalpel and a prayer book.*

*"One of the weaknesses of our age is our apparent
inability to distinguish our needs from
our greeds."*

Don Robinson

I was a greedy drunk. A greedy man. Spoiled,
selfish and demanding. I felt that the world
owed me a living and if I did not get my way,
I sulked, cried or tried to hurt people. And
this greedy attitude to life only made me sad,
dull and boring. Greed, in this sense, could not
work because what I was craving would never
satisfy me.

Then I learned how to "let go". Instead of
demanding, I learned how to wait. Instead of
consuming large amounts of alcohol, I practiced
abstinence. Instead of expecting life on my
terms, I went with the natural flow of life. I
became happy, joyous and free. A miracle? Yes.
I accepted my "needs" and with the acceptance
came the satisfaction.

*Lord, only when I accept my hunger for You am I
truly satisfied.*

*"I respect faith but doubt is what gets you
an education."*

Wilson Mizner

It is okay to question things. It is okay to
say that I do not agree. Today I have the
freedom to doubt opinions and attitudes.

In my childhood I was never allowed to do
this. I had to accept the Bible because the
preacher said it was God's word. I had to accept
that only Christians went to Heaven because
Grandma said so! I had to believe that Jews
and Blacks were "inferior" because family and
friends said so — and to doubt them was to
be different. I was dependent upon an attitude
towards life that I was uncomfortable with. It
brought me pain, anger, loneliness and guilt in
later life.

Then I learned that growth comes to those
who are prepared to doubt or disagree with an
existing system. God is to be found in the
questions. Spirituality is discovered in the
shades of life.

*O God, part of Your glory and splendor is Your
unending mystery.*

"Every dogma has its day, but ideals are eternal."
                                    Israel Zangwill

For too long I lived in a box of rules and dogma. Life had to have definable answers and everything needed to be structured. Then the answers didn't seem to work. Nobody seemed interested in the answers I was giving. The world had moved on!

I realized that life had to be lived, not simply talked about. Having the answers to questions that nobody was asking (including myself) seemed a waste of time. I was uncomfortable. I was living in the past.

Spirituality is reality. It is okay to benefit from a tradition and then move on. I was not disloyal or a traitor because I had changed my mind. God and truth live in a changing world and if we are to grow, our perception of ourselves and life must change. Today I can accept this.

Give me the willingness to change in my life.

*"God cannot be solemn, or he would not have
blessed man with the incalculable gift of laughter."*
Sydney Harris

I think the way to understand God is to
begin to understand man! Sometimes we forget
that we bear the "image" of God — and this
is not so much physical as emotional, our inner
selves, the soul. So much of what I feel, what
hurts me, what causes me distress and pain I
believe also affects God. Also the gifts, the
creative intelligence and spiritual sacrifice that
has characterized so many people in history
reflects something of God. Involved in this is
"laughter". I believe that laughter is derived
from God and is part of the spiritual gift He
has bequeathed to every one of us: we need
only discover it.

"Let go — and let God." Sometimes we need
to get out of our own way so that we can begin
to laugh.

*You gave the gift of laughter to be used. May it be
used in the precious art of healing.*

"Everyone should try to find a spot to be alone."
                        Queen Juliana (Netherlands)

Greta Garbo was reported to have said, "I want to be alone." Life brings its pressures, but we all need to find a place where we can be "alone".

Alone — not to "think" or "do" — simply to be. We need time to simply rest in our lives. A time in the day which we can call our own, to have a visit with the most important person we have got in our lives — ourselves.

To rest in self is to experience "spiritual selfishness" — the joy of self-love.

And how much we look forward to setting aside a time just for heart and mind to center on the pathway to listening to God.

I need to be alone. In my peace I can unite
with You.

*"There is no meaning to life except the meaning
man gives his life by the unfolding of
his powers."*

                                    Eric Fromm

My life was powerless when I was drinking.
The drug alcohol stopped me from reaching my
full potential — I was depressed, tired, angry,
lonely and confused. Incredible as it may sound,
I was the enemy to my life. By drinking alcohol,
I fed the disease and made my life unmanage-
able.

Then I had a "moment" when I saw what
I was doing to my life. The pain caused by
drinking outweighed any advantages. I had hit
my bottom. I began to change my life by
refusing the first drink, and I began to experience a new vitality and potential. A new and
creative life dawned. Friendships and relationships were possible again. God became understandable in His world. My power as a human
being was unleashed in my sobriety.

*Master, may I discover my potential in the loving
decisions I undertake.*

*"We are citizens of the world; and the tragedy of
    our time is that we do not know this."*
                                        Woodrow Wilson

In recovery I have learned to "go home" to
who I am — and part of this involves my
understanding my place in this vast universe.
I am a child of God and my "family" is not
just my immediate blood relatives, but also the
millions of other people that inhabit this
planet.

God did not just make me. God does not
just love me. God is concerned for all His
children. As an alcoholic I did not have this
attitude and I was always feeling lost and
different. I became selfish and narrow in my
lifestyle. Other people were tolerated.

Today I have a "big" God and He has
enabled me to grow not only in my acceptance
of self but also in my acceptance of others.
Today I am a citizen of the world and it feels
good.

*Lord, today I know what it is to belong to the hu-
man family. And with this awareness comes responsibility.*

"To be free is to have achieved your life."
                                        Tennessee Williams

Yesterday's tapes: I need a drink. I can't exist without a fix. How will I get through the morning without taking something? Do people see me shake? Are people watching me? Where can I get money? The prison of addiction!

Today I am free because I took courage and asked for help. Today I am free because I still ask for help. Today I have learned to say "no" to the first drink and life is more comfortable and less painful.

Freedom is a precious spiritual gift that I work for on a daily basis. God is involved — but so am I. The freedom from alcoholism is only guaranteed by the creative choices I make and in the choice is the freedom.

God, my memory is the key to today's freedom;
may I continue to remember.

"Nothing is so much to be feared as fear."
　　　　　　　　　Henry David Thoreau

Fear is a killer. It stops the God-given spirituality in our lives from taking shape and making life enjoyable. Fear is connected with doubt — doubt of self. Low self-esteem develops along with fear and in order for confidence to develop, the fear must be faced, confronted and talked about.

Fear is not going to go away because we wish it away or hope it away or even pray it away. Fear needs to be identified, located and seen for what it is — or, as in most cases, what it isn't. Fear of people, things, tomorrow or life itself grows so long as we forget that we are creatures of God. There is nothing that cannot be faced or overcome — as long as we remain drug-free. God is on our side — but we need also to be on our side. Fear is never stronger than our spirituality. We need to bring our fear into the light; then it can be overcome.

I ask to stay in the light of sobriety, not the darkness of alcoholism.

"Anyone who stops learning is old, whether at twenty or eighty. Anyone who keeps learning stays young. The greatest thing in life is to keep your mind young."

                                Henry Ford

My life is exciting today because I am learning and creating so much in recovery. Even things that I thought I understood have a new "ring". Words, ideas, relationships and the awareness of God are forever changing — usually for the better.

Sobriety is not boring. It is not stuffy, rigid or restrictive — and discussions (not arguments) within the fellowship of recovering people produces fresh insights. Today I am involved in the life of God. I am creating, healing and forever learning more about the mystery of love.

O Teacher of the Universe, let me seek beyond that which I understand.

*"Only a person who can live with himself can
enjoy the gift of leisure."*
                                    Henry Greber

As an addict I could not tolerate my own
company for long. I was forever telephoning
somebody, going over to a friend's house,
inviting people in, creating an "occasion" so
I did not have to think or, at least, think about
myself. Being alone terrified me. I was terrified
because I would begin to think about what was
happening in my life and I did not want to
face it.

Spirituality is reality. Some years ago I
decided to encounter the "real" me, painful
but necessary. I began to develop an awareness
of who I am. Acceptance followed: I am an
alcoholic.

Today I know me; today I like me; today
I can love me — and this awareness brings with
it a knowledge of God, self and my neighbor.

Today I can be alone without feeling lonely.

*"Be still and know that I am God." In this
"stillness" I begin to know myself.*

"Less is more."
                              Mies van der Rohe

As a gambler. I always wanted more. I wanted to win more, get more, have more, spend more — always my energy was in getting "the more". But this constant and demanding lifestyle only gave me less. I could never stop to smell the roses. Activity robbed me of satisfaction. I was running through my life and missing it.

Then somebody told me to stop and rest awhile. Don't chase life; enjoy it. The gambling had become a compulsive and obsessive disease that was ruining my life. I was losing. I was not only losing money — but family, intimacy, life. I was so busy trying to win that I missed the pain and loneliness of my daily losses.

Today I choose not to do this. I accept that the "less" in my life is giving me more. I take responsibility for me, and I share freely with other recovering gamblers.

God, teach me to see Your power and beauty in what I can give up.

*"A great many people think they are thinking
when they are only rearranging their prejudices."*
William James

An aspect of prejudice in my life is my refusal
to listen. I tend to stay with my own thinking
and I "shut off" people or ideas I do not want
to hear. The problem with this attitude is that
it does not lead to discussion, growth or change.

Spirituality is having the capacity to hear
what others are saying, even people you may
not like or respect, and also being prepared to
live with and alongside confusion and "difference". Truth is a many-sided diamond, and it
cannot be comprehended from one viewpoint.
I need to remove my prejudices if I am ever
to move towards an understanding of God's
truth.

I need to learn in my heart that there is
that "image" of God in every person I meet.

*Teach me to listen so that I may hear, so that I
may grow.*

*"Write down the thoughts of the moment. Those
that come unsought are commonly the most
valuable."*

                        Francis Bacon

My mind sometimes races with ideas: What
should I do? What should I write? Where
should I go? Phrases that could prove useful
in an article. People I need to get in contact
with, etc., etc. Many of these ideas come late
at night and so today I have a note pad and
a pencil at the side of my bed so that I can
write down the thought and then go back to
sleep.

I am not God. I know that if I say I will
remember the thought tomorrow, it would be
unrealistic. As an imperfect human being I take
any help I can get. The pad at the side of the
bed is invaluable!

*Let me employ discipline as an aid to joyful and
creative living.*

"The cruelest lies are often told in silence."
                              Robert Louis Stevenson

In treatment I said that I did not "tell" many lies — and although this was not true (hence a lie), it missed the fact that most of my lies were "lies of silence". It was what I did not say that produced the confusion; the pretended self-confidence that hid the pain and shame; the half-spoken truth that harbored the disease.

Communication is the key to any spiritual relationship and a sick silence creates the ultimate blasphemy. God created you and me to relate. In the interchange of our ideas is the miracle born. A sick, angry and ego-centered silence is our shouted "no" to God.

O Lord of the paradox, let me see how the lie of silence can be used to destroy my world.

*"You'll never really know what I mean
and I'll never really know exactly
what you mean."*
                                   Mike Nichols

There is a certain loneliness in life with
which we must all live; perhaps this is the price
of individuality. I am not always sure that I
know what I am feeling or thinking and so I
know I cannot be absolutely sure of what you
are feeling or thinking. Today when I say "I
know how you feel", it is with this reservation.

Another problem I face daily is finding words
to express what I feel — language seems so
inadequate. Words, although bridges to meaning, are often barriers to understanding. What
I mean by what I say is often misunderstood.

This awareness provides me with the stimulus to be more precise, explicit and creative
in my methods of communication and understanding. Today I consider more seriously what
the other person is trying to say, rather than
just listening to the words. Because I am
sensitive to my difficulties in being understood,
I am becoming patient with my neighbor.

Teach us never to become victims of our language.

*"Do not take life too seriously. You will never get
out of it alive."*
                                        Elbert Hubbard

When I used to take life too seriously, I was
always miserable. I missed so much. I placed
a disproportionate amount of energy on my
own importance. I am not saying that I am
not important, but I must learn to live within
the structures of this imperfect world.

For so long I made myself the "victim" of
this world. Every airplane I missed was seen
as a personal abuse. I could not wait in a line
without getting angry and developing a resentment to everybody around. Everybody was
expected to revolve around my world and I felt
the world owed me a living! The result:
unhappiness.

I needed to change or remain unhappy.
Today I am learning to change and I am
working on patience.

*Thank You for the spiritual gift of balance in
my life.*

*"I have offended God and mankind because my
work didn't reach the quality it should have."*
                                        Leonardo da Vinci

How I used to beat myself up! I was not good
enough. I was not attractive enough. I could
not speak properly. I was too small. My family
was not prestigious enough. I was boring. My
breath smelled, etc., etc. I never saw my value
in life. I could never see beyond my failings
into my God-given virtues. Sin was all too
evident in my life!

Today I catch an egotism in my past criticism
of self and others! Who was I to think I should
be perfect? I could find fault with the Arch-
angel Gabriel if he came to be my neighbor.
My compulsive disease extended beyond drugs
to negative attitudes about life.

Today I see my value. Sobriety has restored
my dignity. Today I am in touch with that part
of me that is noble. Today in my sobriety I
am a spiritual somebody, not a nobody.

*Let my desire for "perfection" be tempered
by reality.*

"Integrity has no need of rules."
                              Albert Camus

The benefit of a spiritual program is the development of integrity in my life. Integrity is having an honest respect for myself; it is respecting who I am and how I live in the world. Integrity also becomes a bridge by which I can reach my fellow man. My respect for my life develops a respect for others. My determination to have integrity affects the way I treat you. Integrity gives me freedom to be — and this allows for an acceptance of you.

Of course I must follow some rules and guidelines in my life but today they are not written in cement. Today I can be flexible with me and this means that I can be flexible with you. My past need to control has developed into an accepting serenity that brings peace. My spiritual program forever teaches me to be free; now I can live.

I pray that I can see beyond the rules into the beauty of Integrity.

> *"In the republic of mediocrity, genius is*
> *dangerous."*
> *Robert G. Ingersoll*

Spirituality is a creative and positive energy that forever seeks new ways to improve and heal itself. Spirituality is never satisfied with mediocrity. God is alive in musicians, writers, singers and prophets — and always the standard of "excellence" is searched for; best can be made better!

As a drunk I often settled for convenience, "no sweat", mediocrity. My motto was "Why bother?". "It can be done tomorrow." I had low energy. Addiction robs the human being of God's productive energy.

In recovery I seek the best because I believe I am the best; God made me — and I respect His choice!

Lord, save me from the "comfortable way" that
makes no demands on my genius.

"The devil can cite scripture for his purpose."
                    William Shakespeare

This quotation reminds me that the disease of alcoholism is "cunning, baffling and powerful". I am aware of the need to walk like I talk, to make the action fit the word, to live my program today rather than talk about it for tomorrow. Why? Because the disease can talk program! I have caught myself saying things that I do not practice in my life. I catch myself saying things to others that I do not live out in my own life. Today I am aware of my hypocrisy. Today I am aware of the disease in my life.

I need to be aware of this aspect of the disease because I am such a good talker, such a convincing talker, such a practiced manipulator! Today I know that I am not perfect, but that should never be an excuse to avoid dealing with my character defects. I must not "con" myself into staying sick!

I pray that I may strive to live the message.

*"One of the disadvantages of wine is that it makes
a man mistake words for thoughts."*
                                        Samuel Johnson

Alcohol produced problems in my life. I was
unable to control my drinking and the result
was catastrophe. I hurt people. I endangered
my health. I ruined my productivity. I became
lonely. I felt isolated. I was forever getting into
arguments. The police were often involved.
People who loved me had to walk away from
me for their own sanity. Alcohol made my life
a mess!

Today I can see this and I am glad I made
the spiritual decision to refuse the first drink.
Today I am getting my life together. I am
becoming a productive citizen. I have friends
and relationships again. But I need to remember what I must never forget:

Alcohol + Me = Problems.

Lord, alcohol is a gift I can refuse.

*"We should be careful to get out of an experience
only the wisdom that is in it."*
Mark Twain

I need to risk in life. I need to try again.
I need to face life and not run from it. Early
in my sobriety I was scared to try new things
because I was afraid I might get hurt. I was
afraid to express my feelings. I hid in the idea
of simply "not drinking".

Spirituality is about being willing to reach
out into new areas, engage in new and different
relationships, enjoy the richness of God's
world. As I grow in sobriety I develop the
capacity to react differently to painful situations and overcome them. I learn that mistakes
can make for new conquests. That lasting joys
and achievements are born in the risk.

*Teach me to overcome yesterday's sorrows with
today's optimism.*

*"The one serious conviction that a man should
have is that nothing is to be taken seriously."*
         Nicholas Murray Butler

For years I used to take myself too seriously.
I thought that everything depended upon my
thoughts, actions and decisions. Life was a
series of agendas that had to be met; life was
too serious to be joked about. I knew that I
was not God, but I took responsibility for the
whole universe. I had opinions on everything
and everybody and I was, of course, always
right.

As the years passed it grew painful being so
responsible — my control produced stress,
tension and loneliness. Then a friend said to
me, "Let go and let God." I began to detach
and laugh at my insane behavior. I laughed
more as I began to accept my humanness. I
discovered spirituality in the joke. God must
have a sense of humor — after all, He made
me.

*Help me to laugh at myself in my search for
the Kingdom.*

*Let there be
spaces
in your
togetherness.*

Kahlil Gibran

"Seek not to understand that you may believe, but believe that you understand."
> *St. Augustine*

For years I tried to understand my behavior around alcohol and I only came away more confused. Sometimes my efforts to understand led me into dishonesty and manipulation. I drank because I was lonely, angry, happy, overworked or because I had problems with my parents. You see, I tried to understand "why"!

Science has no definitive answer as to why some people are alcoholic other than to postulate the disease factor, with the emphasized advice, "Don't pick up the first drink." So today I don't understand why I am an alcoholic. I also believe that I can never drink alcohol without having alcohol problems. This cherished belief keeps me sober and gives me a God I can understand; a life that I can love; and I world I can live in.

Oh yes — and I can remember where I have been today!

Help me to believe in what I know and to be content with the imperfection of my knowledge.

*"There is a paradox in pride: it makes some men
ridiculous, but prevents some men from
becoming so."*
Charles Caleb Colton

Pride can be both negative and creative. I
have experienced both in my alcoholic life.
When I was drinking, my pride made me an
arrogant fool, refusing to listen to the advice
of others, always telling people what they
should do, unrealistic in my demands on myself
and others, lost in a fantasy of how I appeared
to others. Pride became a mask behind which
I hid my feelings.

In recovery I am beginning to develop a love
and respect for myself. I am proud of my
achievements in recovery, and I am beginning
to discover the "power" God has given to me.
My spiritual program teaches me that I need
to cooperate with God if things are going to
happen in my life. God requires my involvement if He is to work through my life. Today
I am proud of my willingness to associate with
the God of Truth.

*Master, let me always treat "pride" with respect,
mindful of its destructive attributes.*

*"Destiny is not a matter of chance, it is a matter
of choice; it is not a thing to be achieved."*
William Jennings Bryan

It is so important for us to see that we create
our destiny. We create our futures in the
choices we initiate today. During my addiction
I was like a ship without a sail. I drifted through
life and was tossed in a thousand directions.
Today I am able to point myself in the direction
I want to go.

I do not believe that this attitude takes
anything away from the power of God because
He gave me freedom in the first place! He
created me to be free and to have the gift of
decision-making. He is not a dictator God, and
I am not a puppet on a string. He loves me
enough to allow me to learn from my mistakes
and take personal pride in my achievements.
Addiction made me powerless. Sobriety puts
me in touch with my God-given power.

*I am forever grateful and thankful for my
involvement in my own life. I pray today
that I might live responsibly
a day at a time.*

"Freedom is nothing else but a chance to be better."
Albert Camus

Human beings are not puppets. Sometimes when you hear people talk about God and prayer, they imply that we have no choice and that all actions in life are determined by God alone: a moment's reflection should make us hesitate from such a viewpoint. Murder, rape, child molestation and prejudice do not stem from God but are the results of God's gift of freedom to mankind.

Addicts and alcoholics need to comprehend on a daily basis that prayers that are not accompanied by actions are mere words. God's love for man does not obliterate man's need to love himself through choice and decision. Sobriety and serenity should be experienced in our lives when divinity is revealed in our choice.

God, help me to appreciate my involvement in my desire to be a winner.

"Without forgiveness life is governed by . . . an
endless cycle of resentment and retaliation."
Roberto Assagioli

So much of what I resent in others springs
from my unhappiness with self. I hate in others
what I know to be in myself: arrogance, pride,
narrow-mindedness, snobbery and dishonesty.

Today I am learning that as long as I refuse
to forgive others, I am not capable of forgiving
myself. Part of my denial is reflected in my
attitudes towards others. Those character traits
I refuse to forgive in others are buried within
myself. I know that without forgiveness there
is no freedom — and I wish to grow in freedom.

Today I am learning the difference between
forgiveness and acceptance. I can forgive other
people without accepting their lifestyle. I can
forgive myself and still see the need for change.
In my forgiveness is the hope for tomorrow.

Master, You taught that without forgiveness,
there can be no pure love. Help me grow in the
forgiveness of self and others.

> *"The measure of man is what he does
> with power."*
>
> > *Pittacus*

With my recovery has come a certain success, and with that success comes power. Power comes with the spiritual program, but it must be exercised responsibly. Just as the disease used alcohol to destroy my life, so it can use power to destroy me in sobriety. Power is a double-edged sword that has led many back to drinking. Certainly an abuse of power is not consistent with sobriety.

Today I am respectful of power because I know it can lead to an inflated ego or an arrogant personality that continues to destroy the quality of life. Today I surround myself with friends who will remind me of my roots.

Teach me not to use my White Anglo-Saxon Protestant heritage to belittle or patronize those from minority groups.

Teach me to exercise power responsibly.

"Doubt isn't the opposite of faith; it is an element of faith."

Paul Tillich

That part of me that does not know is vibrant in spirituality. Problems are part of what it is to be human and an element of doubt is essential. With the doubt comes the growth.

However, as a younger man I was told that it was a sin to doubt; God demanded a steadfast faith and doubt could have no part of faith! I remember going to confession and feeling guilty and ashamed about my doubts — but I did doubt and doubt has always played a part in my life. In some ways I think that my religious doubts have been the most creative part of me — certainly they have enabled me to grow and build a bridge of understanding with others.

Master, hear, through the doubts, my love of You.

"There is no must in art because it is free."
                                        Vasily Kandinsky

Now I understand why the religious people of the past persecuted the artist. Now I understand why so many artists moved away from religion and grew beyond it. The artist is always searching for that which is different, that which cannot be contained or codified; that which is free: Spirituality.

As a drinking alcoholic I found it necessary to control my life; control my thoughts and behavior; control each and every situation — and it was depressingly exhausting. Today sobriety enables me to risk that which is new and different. Sobriety allows me to experiment and take risks in God's world. Sobriety is being free.

I am discovering more of me in what yesterday's artists wrote and produced. The "musts" of yesterday have been replaced by the shoulds and needs of today. I am free to listen and consider the person because he is a person and not simply because of his credentials.

Supreme Artist, let me hear You in the
whisperings of Your creatures.

"There is no sadder sight than a young pessimist."
                                    Mark Twain

I meet so many young people who have "aged" because of their drug addiction. They have lost that "spark" of youth that is both creative and hopeful. They reveal in their eyes a "powerlessness" that keeps them prisoners of lethargy. They don't want to do anything. They mumble rather than speak. They walk with no purpose: young zombies! Addiction breeds pessimism.

Recovery is realizing that life need not be like this. True joy and happiness comes with the experience of self, rather than the confused experiences of chemicals. Reality is facing the pain and problems in order to rediscover the dynamic spirituality of a drug-free life. The "yes" to life begins with the "no" to drugs. Happiness and confidence are discovered in the "yes" to life.

Let me see beyond the gloom to the promised
sunrise of tomorrow.

*"Must the hunger become anger and the anger
become fury before anything will be done?"*
                                    John Steinbeck

I have a gratitude in my life today that stems
from the daily recovery I enjoy in my life.
Today I am happy, joyous and content; I am
able to deal with the daily problems that we
all have to face. I am grateful that I have a
disease that it is possible to recover from.

However, there are millions of people who
suffer in poverty or with diseases that cannot
be "arrested" by a change in behavior or
attitude: What can I do for these people?

Well, I can seek to pray for them daily. I
can visit them or comfort their families when
the opportunity arises. But more than this I
can give money to the various research foun-
dations that exist and require the support of
the public. I have an awareness of my need
to give. My feeling of gratitude must be earthed
in the support of practical charities.

Lord, let the gratitude I feel enable me to give.

*"The foolish and the dead never change
their opinion."*
James Russell Lowell

Part of my understanding of spirituality is
that I will change. I will change my mind, my
attitude and my opinion. My understanding of
sobriety is that I will grow, grow in an understanding of myself, grow in an understanding
of God's will for me, and grow in an understanding of other people. Today I am not afraid
to change my thinking about life.

During my years as an addict I was fixed and
rigid about everything. I saw it as weakness to
change my mind and opinions. Now I understand that I was afraid of change, afraid not
to have an answer, afraid not to be seen as
being "in charge".

In treatment I learned how to understand
spirituality as reality; seeing things as they are,
rather than how I wanted them to be. I began
to accept that life is about change and that
truth is a process that we evolve towards.

*In my journey towards You may I have the
willingness to change.*

"Violence is counter-productive and produces changes of a sort you don't want. It is a very dangerous instrument and can destroy those who wield it."

John Gardner

I believed I wasn't violent when I drank but that is not true; I wasn't physically violent but I used emotional and mental violence. I did not hit, fight or mutilate people with my hands, but I could tear a person apart with my tongue. My sarcasm and criticism made people cry, feel demoralized and useless. Violence always removes the "dignity" from man — and I did this with my mouth!

Today I try to practice tolerance and patience. I count to ten, and when I do lose my temper and hurt a person unfairly or unnecessarily, I apologize. In my sobriety the anger, hate and need to hurt is slowly going. I am progressively getting better a day at a time.

Teacher, let me offer the hand of peace, not the fist of violence.

*"To behave with dignity is nothing less than to
allow others freely to be themselves."*
Sol Chaneles

I believe that ultimately I can only be
responsible for me. It is impossible for me to
live another person's life. It is disrespectful to
assume the role of decision-maker for another
adult human being. People must have the
freedom to grow and be themselves. Dignity
is affording people this freedom.

Today I can see how I continued to keep
members of my family sick by taking on a
responsibility that was not mine. I can see how
I was not giving dignity to my family; I was
unintentionally withholding dignity from those
I loved. People, especially family members, must
be given the freedom to express their hurts.
They have a responsibility to deal with their
pain — because it is theirs!

*I pray that I may give to others the dignity I desire
in my own life.*

"The ability to accept responsibility is the measure of the man."

                               Roy L. Smith

I believe the greatest insight into my life is that I am responsible; my responsibility is an important and dignified gift from God. My responsibility reveals my involvement in God's creation, in my life and my recovery from alcoholism. Greatness is in the choices I make, and the choices come with God's gift of freedom. Human beings are more than puppets on a string or automated machines. We are creative creatures who carry the burden and joy of responsibility.

Along with the acceptance of my alcoholism I also accepted the responsibility to remain sober in my decisions and lifestyle: such is greatness.

Thank You for giving me the responsibility to co-create with You.

*"I know that the twelve notes in each octave and
the varieties of rhythm offer me opportunities that
all of human genius will never exhaust."*
                                    Igor Stravinsky

There is so much to be gained in life. Just
when you think you have exhausted all pos-
sibilities, a new insight is perceived, permuta-
tions and varieties appear in abundance. An
example is sobriety. I thought it meant not
drinking but today I see that it affects all areas
of my life — how I walk, the hugs I freely give,
my acceptance of others, my willingness to
trust and risk, my optimism for a new day.

Also God is comprehensive for me today. He
is alive in church, the Bible and tradition but
He is also alive in literature, scripture, sexuality
and music. Today I can hear beyond the
symphony into the unfathomable message of
God's love for His creation. And always I hear
something different and new.

*Thank You, Lord, for Your messengers who love
through the art of music.*

"One must not lose desires. They are mighty
stimulating to creativeness, to love,
and to long life."
                            Alexander A. Bogomoletz

Today I desire to live. I have discovered value
in my life. I have experienced personal self-
esteem. I am able to feel again, talk, trust and
laugh again. Today I desire to live.

But I can remember when I felt lonely,
isolated, angry, shutdown and hopeless. The
desires I had were destructive, desiring isolation
mingled with alcohol. Then the pain became
too great and I experienced a vital "moment".
I realized I needed to make a choice — was
I to live or die? I chose to live!

This was the beginning of my spiritual
journey into self from which I discovered God
and His world. Creative and positive desires
were re-born in my life, and I am able to live
and love again.

O Lord, may I continue to desire those things that
do not hurt me.

"My life has been nothing but a failure."
Claude Monet

I can identify with Claude Monet because for years I considered myself a complete failure. For years I wallowed on my pity-pot until it became too painful. Whatever the "pay-off" was in the previous years had dried up, and I was left with a rock bottom pain that forced me to consider the alternative: I needed to set about doing something to change things!

Astounding! Impossible! How could this ever be? I was forever to be a victim of alcoholism.

"Not so." I heard a voice of hope from a recovering alcoholic who had made the change. Slowly I took small steps towards recovery and self-esteem.

I am a failure so long as I consider myself a failure. I am what I create in my life. God requires my cooperation to make miracles in my life. My decision to listen to those who had achieved sobriety provided the seeds for my recovery today. I wonder if Claude Monet was an alcoholic who never heard the words of hope?

Lord, the only real failure is not seeing You in our lives.

*"It is well for a man to respect his own vocation,
whatever it is, and to think himself bound to
uphold it and to claim for it the
respect it deserves."*

Charles Dickens

Nobody else is quite like me. Nobody else can view the world, experience the world, feel the world in the way that I can. I am the center of the universe. Other people can love — but it is not the same as my love. Other people can offer the hand of friendship — but it is not the same as the friendship that I can offer. Other people can utter a kind word — but the phrasing of my words belong to me. I am unique and I must remember that. Even my space in the world is special. Nobody can take up the place that I have on the earth; you cannot get into my space. We may both be looking at the same scene, but I see it from my place in the world. Today I respect my uniqueness.

*Let me continue to discover something of Your
unique image in my life.*

"We are none of us infallible — not even the youngest of us."

W. H. Thompson

When I was a young man I did not want to listen to older people because I felt that they did not understand me. With hindsight I see that I did not want to hear what they were saying about my lifestyle.

Today now that I am a "mature man" with a few years of sobriety, I must avoid having the same attitude towards the young, not listening to them because I think they are "too young" or do not understand! I must not repeat, in reverse, yesterday's mistakes!

None of us are infallible. We are not God. We can learn from each other if we have the patience to listen. Sometimes we need to seek the meaning behind the words.

God, teach me to listen with the ear of understanding and patience.

> *"When I look back on all these worries,*
> *I remember the story of the old man*
> *who said on his deathbed that he had*
> *had a lot of trouble in his life,*
> *most of which never happened."*
>
> Winston Churchill

I know I can worry myself into the grave.
I can project an incident into a calamity. I can
make mountains out of molehills.

I worried about what people meant by what
they said; I always looked for a hidden criticism;
I worried about what people did not say; I
worried about what people were thinking or
were going to do or were plotting. If I had
nothing to worry about, then I worried because
I felt I should have something to worry about!
I created most of the worry in my life.

Today I have a program that helps me deal
with this. Of course I still worry, but I have
a "checklist" that keeps me sane and allows
me to laugh at the insanity of my projections.
Today the worry in my life is less destructive
and negative.

Let me bring my worry to You in prayer.
Then let me sleep!

"Not ignorance, but ignorance of ignorance is the death of knowledge."
                    Alfred North Whitehead

How little I understood when I was living as an alcoholic. How little I wanted to know. Ignorance was bliss in my addiction. And the real tragedy was that I was ignorant of the extent of my ignorance! I had no idea how serious my alcoholism was, how pervasive in all areas of my life it had developed, how destructive and negative I had become until I was made to "see" reality in treatment. Reluctantly I opened my eyes to see my ignorance and I knew I needed to change my attitude if I was to recover.

The enemy of the spiritual life is ignorance because it stops us from realizing that the strength and healing power of spirituality has been given by God — all we need do is discover it and appreciate it.

I pray that I and others will have the courage to confront the ignorance in my life.

*"It is not death that a man should fear, but he
should fear never beginning to live."*
                                    Marcus Aurelius

For years I did not live I simply existed. What
many people take for granted I did not have:
friends, vacations, job satisfaction, gratitude,
family, communication and love of self. An
aspect of my disease, my denial, was that I
thought I was happy without having any
evidence for such a feeling. Indeed, my lifestyle
indicated progressive isolation. That's illusion.
A recovering alcoholic priest shared that early
in recovery he saw a sunset and remarked,
"How long has that been happening?" Like
him, I missed so much!

Life is to be lived or endured. My spiritual
recovery means that every day I reach out to
life and grasp it, hold it, smell it — and smile.

*God of life, let me live today. Let my "high" be the
glory of the day.*

*"The only question with wealth is what you do
with it."*
                              John D. Rockefeller, Jr.

Prosperity, if it is truly to be appreciated,
needs to be shared. Wealth only makes sense
when it is put to use for the benefit of the
many. To horde treasure is to miss the value
of that treasure. Money makes the world go
around but it can only produce joy and
excitement when it is spent or put to work.

This is also true for those who have a
"wealth" of ideas or talents — they need to
be expressed, shared and valued by others to
be of any real benefit. A writer needs to write,
a musician needs to play, a painter demands
a canvas — and the world needs to appreciate.

God is at work in His world and He requires
recognition.

*Let me find You in the talents that You have
shared with me.*

"This great misfortune — to be incapable
of solitude."

Jean de la Bruyere

Today I am able to live with my loneliness.
I know the difference between being "alone"
and being "lonely" — and even in sobriety I
experience loneliness. But today I can live with
it.

When I was drinking, I had an overwhelming
feeling of being lost and isolated; today it is
tolerable. I can live with it. It is part of being
"imperfect". I am not God.

The reality of spirituality demands that I do
not escape into a fantasy that denies my
feelings of loneliness. It is part of my journey
towards God. I will never appreciate perfect
happiness until I rest in God. This I accept.
In sobriety I have many days of happiness and
moments of joy — but I am, at times, lonely
— with feelings of being lost. Today I can
accept this — and talk about it.

I accept that part of me will be forever lost until I
rest in God.

*"Experience has taught me this, that we undo
ourselves by impatience. Misfortunes have their
life and their limits, their sickness
and their health."*
                    Michel de Montaigne

Nothing lasts forever. At times I feel sad,
angry, resentful and ashamed — but it passes.
In my recovery I have learned to live in "my
day" and accept the consequences of that day.
I can only deal with life as I experience it.
Tomorrow is a new day with new experiences.
And some of the experiences are painful.
Reality teaches me this. At times I wish I could
go through life without pain or rejection but
I know that is fantasy. Sobriety does not mean
that everything will be perfect — only better!

Nothing is so bad that I need to drink or
use over it. Today I know that alcohol increases
my pain; it is never a solution. God, who has
given me today, will also give me a tomorrow
— and time eases the pain if I work my
program. Misfortunes are not worth drinking
over. Nothing lasts forever.

Thank You for the gift of a tomorrow.

"Adversity reveals genius, prosperity conceals it."
                                          Horace

Today I believe that the only way to understand God, the world, my neighbor and
myself is through some degree of suffering. Pain
and suffering are humbling in the truest sense;
they stop you from being arrogant, selfish and
"prideful".

I know this because I was a spoiled child.
My family tried to give me everything. Whatever I wanted was given to me; my way or no
way! This sick love robbed me of humility and
separated me from humanity: it made me feel
different, selfish and placed me on a pity-pot.
Being spoiled stopped me experiencing the real
world and stopped me from growing.

Today adversity is part of life and part of
being human. Not to grow through adversity
is to die. To have everything is to experience
nothing. To feel in life — to have emotion
— demands adversity and pain.

*Teach me to be grateful for the suffering that leads
to growth.*

"Ideas shape the course of history."
                              John Maynard Keynes

I get so excited about my sobriety because it has given me ideas. Today I can think, ponder and create. God is such a big idea today — everything is involved.

For years I had made God a prisoner of the Church or an idea in history, but in my sobriety I have discovered Him in art, poetry, music and literature. God is found in friendship, advice, sharing and sexuality. God is forcibly experienced in nature, sunsets, animals and the sea.

God can be found through my failures. He is perceived in suffering, loneliness and resentments. The acknowledgment of my disease has brought me closer to God as I understand Him.

My idea of God is alive and it makes me want to live.

*May my ideas and thoughts always reflect
Your beauty.*

*"Whatever you may be sure of, be sure of this —
that you are dreadfully like other people."*
                                    James Russell Lowell

For many years I saw the differences and not the similarities. I was always considering how I was unlike other alcoholics, rather than perceiving the striking similarities. I kept myself on the outside, not only in recovery from alcoholism but also in life.

Then I heard from another recovering alcoholic not only "my story" but also my feelings. My armor of denial was broken down. I realized I belonged. I was with people who knew my loneliness, isolation, confusion, guilt and despair. I had come home to live amongst my people.

Thank You for enabling me to see that I am a member of the human family and a recovering alcoholic.

"I determine who is a Jew."
Hermann Goering

Playing God. How well I remember this attitude in my drinking days when, because I had said it, it must be so! Arrogance and pride kept me lonely and isolated.

Today my spiritual program teaches me to "play" God in a different way. It requires that I seek to discover the values I associate with God and live them out in my own life. Because I believe that God is loving and accepting, I seek to reveal these qualities in my daily associations. It makes no sense to worship a God of truth if I continue the life of "the liar". Belief must determine change.

As a recovering alcoholic I seek to "play" God in the joy, acceptance and love I show to myself and other people. However, I know (oh how I know!) that I am not God!

Let my statements always be open to the "pure light" of change.

"Hear the meaning within the word."
                                    William Shakespeare

When I hear or see the word "sobriety", I am made to think of relationships: my relationship with God, man and, more importantly, myself. Sobriety means humor, hope and joy. It means a silence at the center of my being that "wonders" at it all. Sobriety means a sexuality that is both noble and free — that risks rejection and criticism. Sobriety argues against prejudice and bigotry. It builds a bridge to "the different" and reflects on the creative variety of man. It allows me a God as I understand Him but also respects tradition and the ancient philosophies of the world.

Sobriety evokes a feeling that is beyond words. It echoes the spiritual life.

Let me learn to pray beyond words. Let my relationship with You grow in silence.

"What makes resisting temptation difficult for many people is that they don't want to discourage it completely."

Franklin P. Jones

Usually I am tempted because I want to be. I allow myself to get too close to the object of my desire or I invite the problem into my life knowing that I will not resist it. Then I use my "imperfection" as an excuse! In this way I manipulate my spiritual program and become dishonest.

When I first got sober, I did not allow alcohol in my house; I did not go to bars; I did not spend time with heavy drinkers; I avoided airplanes or places that I would associate with alcohol. This disciplined approach to sobriety worked. If you don't invite the enemy in, you won't get beaten up. I need to continue to remember these simple rules and not get complacent in my sobriety.

Let me keep temptation out of my life by avoiding it.

"The way to greatness is the path of self-reliance, independence and steadfastness in times of trial and stress."

                           Herbert Hoover

Today I take responsibility for my life. Today I take responsibility for my disease. Today I take responsibility for my recovery. I know I am not perfect and I have many pains and problems yet to face, but I take hope in my daily conquests. Nothing is too great for me to overcome so long as I have confidence in myself. It is my "yes" or "no" that makes the difference. In the power of my choice rests my freedom.

God, I thank You for my daily trials that ensure my victories.

"Nobody ever died of laughter."
                                Max Beerbohm

I knew that I was growing in self-esteem and confidence when I was able to laugh, express that "belly" laugh that proclaims that I am glad to be alive.

So many religious people are too serious. They seem to think that God disapproves of laughter and yet it seems the most natural emotion in the world. Sobriety is a statement that the pain is being overcome and the hope that is experienced will necessarily release laughter.

Laughter also stops us from treating ourselves and the world too seriously. I remember a professor telling me, "God created the world for fun. Find the key to life and enjoy it." Spirituality is that key.

Sometimes, Lord, in the silence of my car, my joy is so great and my gratitude so overwhelming, I can do nothing but laugh. Thank You for the gift of laughter.

"Man — a being in search of meaning."
                                    Plato

Today I am on my way. With my sobriety has come a desire to understand — understand life, understand me, understand my relationships and understand God. Meaning — what is true? What is noble? What is spiritual? These are important to me today.

I no longer wish to hurt, damage, ridicule, destroy, fight, lie or cheat in my life. I've had enough of being negative. I've had enough of being lost and isolated in my arrogance. I've had enough of standing on the outside of life, feeling resentful and afraid.

Sobriety, for me today, involves my search for meaning — knowing full well that my understanding will always be imperfect and I can never comprehend fully. The ultimate answer is in living with confusion. I am not God . . . but I still intend to reach for the stars.

Lord, my cry for self-awareness is answered in the journey and not the destination.

"Education is helping the child realize his
potentialities."
                                        Eric Fromm

When I was drinking, I behaved like a child. I behaved not just like a child but "childish". I was so dependent upon my alcohol, so addicted, that I never realized my potential in life. I never realized the gift of life!

Today I have a spiritual program that offers me the world; it sets no limits on my horizons; it encourages me to discover my potential and live it. Today I am learning new languages, visiting different countries and enjoying alternative cultures, making new friendships and, most importantly, discovering the "bigness" of God in His world. The education I have gained in my sobriety seems unending and unstoppable. Each day produces a new opportunity and a different experience. Everyday is a time to receive.

Teach me to journey through the words into the
experience.

"Thought makes the whole dignity of man;
therefore endeavor to think well, that is
the only morality."

Blaise Pascal

I think that human beings are very imitative creatures; we imitate clothes, hair styles, mannerisms and lifestyles. A man's mind will be influenced by what he listens to and what he reads. And what we think is very important to sobriety.

Today I make an effort to examine my thinking and check it out with a sponsor or in a support group. I know that my dignity in sobriety is connected not only with what I do but also with my attitudes and thoughts — when my thinking begins to go crazy, I know I am in a dangerous place and I need to talk. God created me with the ability to think, therefore, I need to safeguard the information I put in my mind.

Let me learn to develop morality of mind.

*"If the blind lead the blind, both shall fall into
the ditch."*
                              Jesus (Matthew 15:14)

I need to understand before I can teach; I
need to listen before I give advice; I need to
associate myself with the "winners" to become
a winner.

For years I sought advice and direction from
those who did not understand. They tried to
help but they did not understand. Today I
understand that part of my denial and manipulation was choosing those who did not understand to help me. This way I could stay sick!

My spiritual journey involves seeking out
those who have that "something" that I want
— and being willing to follow their directions;
I surrender to live.

*Teach me to develop the spiritual ego that
is teachable.*

"There is no more evil thing in the world than race prejudice . . . It justifies and holds together more baseness, cruelty and abomination than any other sort of error in the world."

H. G. Wells

Something about me fears racism because I know that I am at risk. If a group of people can be persecuted or ridiculed for being "different" from others, then why shouldn't it eventually happen to me? With racism the whole world is at risk.

Also racism is the opposite of spirituality. Spirituality always seeks to include, bring together and unite. The world that God has made is ONE. All people and races are "a family" that must learn to co-exist together if we are to be productive and creative. In the variety is the strength. With the unusual and peculiar comes divinity. God is to be found in the confusions of life.

Teacher, let me have the courage to expose the inadequacies in my life.

> *"Money often costs too much."*
> *Ralph Waldo Emerson*

Money can be a curse. It can destroy people. Money in itself has no value. It needs to be "used" or "put to work". The problem is that many people think it can work miracles, i.e., "make me happy", "give me self-esteem", "bring love into my life", "remove my loneliness", "cure my insecurities and remove my alcohol or drug problems!" The historical list of wealthy casualties indicates that this is not the case. We cannot "buy" ourself out of a disease! In this sense, money costs too much.

Because I have a compulsive nature, I need to be aware of my desire for money and the responsible way I need to use it. Spirituality involves the use of money. I need to be positive in my attitude towards money but also creative about how to use it.

I need always to remember that true wealth is found in my discovery of the God within and not in the clothes I wear.

O God, let me make money serve me; may I never be foolish enough to serve it.

*"The man who has become a thinking being feels a
compulsion to give to every creature the same
reverence for life that he gives to his own."*
                                    Albert Schweitzer

Today I accept people. Even the people with
whom I do not agree, I accept. My freedom
is dependent upon my attitude towards others.
My respect is rooted in the respect I give to
others. God is to be found in my neighbor!

Nowhere is this more true for me as a
religious person than in my attitude to people
of other creeds — and those who have none!
The spiritual life that unites me to God and
the world requires not only my acceptance of
"difference" but my personal need for it.

But more than this; even those who hurt,
abuse and destroy need to be accepted from
within my spiritual self — because something
of their life exists in mine. In this accepting
love is the daily healing of my disease.

*May my acceptance of the tyrant lead to the
forgiveness of the self.*

*"Faith must trample underfoot all reason, sense
and understanding."*
                                    Martin Luther

An obstacle to my understanding the spiritual life was my intellectualization; my head was forever getting in the way of my heart. It was much easier for me to think, rather than to feel; my faith was smothered by logic. My manipulating and controlling mind was stopping me experiencing the adventure of faith.

The poet in me grew as I began to trust others. God became alive in my confusion. The answer was in not having to have the answers. Today spirituality involves all the varied confusions and paradoxes of life that I have discovered in me and in others — and it's okay.

Today the love I give and receive is beyond my wildest dreams, and I smile at the joy of my confusion.

*May my head unite with my heart in the
daily maze of life.*

*"The race advances only by the extra achievements
of the individual. You are the individual."*
                                    Charles Towne

The spiritual program that involves a "love
of self" has made me get in touch with my
individuality. Although we can identify with
other people's feelings and situations, we are
also not exactly the same. Our dreams and
aspirations are different, our gifts and achievements vary, our personal individuality adds to
the variety of life.

My "difference" needs to be nurtured
alongside my spiritual growth, especially since
being a recovering alcoholic I am tempted to
"please" the crowd. Today my personal inventory revolves around my needs, hopes and
dreams that are realistic. Spirituality is reality.

In helping myself to the abundant richness
that is within me, I am contributing to society
and the world.

*Thank You for making the world with such
creative difference; may I continue to risk
in this knowledge.*

"The tragedy of life is what dies in man while he lives."

                             Albert Schweitzer

Addiction progressively takes away the vitality of life. It robs life of meaning. Addiction isolates; it kills by atrophy. People, places and things lose meaning; everything becomes a chore and God is lost. We say to compensate that we are having "fun" — we say this a lot and at times we believe it, but in the silence of the night we know it to be a lie.

We lie to others and to ourselves. Sometimes we believe the lie! At this point we begin to die unless we take courage and confront "the lie" in order to live.

Today I live because I confronted my lie. I have discovered the spiritual power that was buried deep beneath the progressive addiction. And I am finding it easier and less painful to live.

May I continue to breathe a daily "yes" in my life so that I might live.

"Humankind cannot bear very much reality."
                                          T. S. Eliot

I wonder why we find it hard to face reality?
I preferred to escape from my problems, avoid
who I was, not deal with the issues of God,
relationships or loneliness — and live in a world
of "make believe". However, it did not work.
The pain of being a "fake" and living a lie
became too great so I asked for help.

Today I am on a journey towards reality and
it is a spiritual journey. I know I will never
be completely real. A part of me will always
be "diseased". I must live and treat my
compulsive behavior on a daily basis — but
my life is getting better, and I am slowly growing
in an understanding of who I am and what I
need.

God, let me be as real as I can be.

*"If error is corrected whenever it is recognized as
such, the path of error is the path of truth."*
                              Hans Reichenbach

I believe that in order to discover spirituality
in our lives, we need to confront the "disease",
that destructive and negative side of our lives.
We need to make the disease work for us!

For too many years I tried to avoid and deny
my alcoholism. I wanted to recover by osmosis!
I did not want to get my hands dirty with the
reality of my suffering but rather I wanted a
"miracle" — really magic — to make everything different from what it had been for years.
I did not want to face my pain! But it does
not work that way. If I am to get well, I need
to confront my disease, smell my disease, hold
my disease, pull and tug at the disease in my
life. Why? Because it is mine. I need to be in
touch with my disease if I am ever going to
make the necessary changes. I need to make
my disease work for me — that is spirituality.

*Let me have the courage to pass through the pain
in order to experience the gain.*

*"Property is the fruit of labor; property is
desirable; it is a positive good."*
                                                  Abraham Lincoln

God is to be found in the physical. He is
to be found in my body, my sexuality, the
mountains and streams — and also in houses
and real estate. The luxury of comfort and good
living is not incompatible with the spiritual life
— indeed, the use of our property can be an
opportunity for gratitude and sharing.

I know many people who use their comfortable homes for opportunities to develop sincere
friendships. Luxury homes can be used for
retreats and spiritual seminars involving music,
dance and silence. Property is part of God's
landscape in this world. His love, joy and hope
for mankind can be experienced by our creative
use of property.

Let me use my property creatively.

*"To believe in sensible ideas is easy, but to
   implement them involves sacrifice."*
                                    Dorothy Fosdick

What am I prepared to sacrifice for what
I want? I remember the time I said I would
do "anything". Today I know that anything
must be translated into something. No person,
job or thing can be allowed to come between
myself and abstinence. This love of self will
enable me to love others. But I must remember
to sacrifice my desire to please others and place
my needs as a priority in my life.

Today I know that if I do not love myself
enough to make sacrifices, then I can be
nothing.

*In gratitude I give up those things I know will
hurt me.*

*"Nothing will ever be attempted if all possible
objections must be first overcome."*
Samuel Johnson

There was a time when I never attempted anything because I said it "can't" be done. I could never get sober. I could never stand up to my drunken friends. I could never face my buried secrets. I could never stop gambling. I could never change my eating habits or stop using cocaine.

Then I heard the confidence and hope that was reflected in people who were recovering from these same problems. I heard people talk about what it was like, what happened and what it is like now. They told me I didn't mean "can't", I meant "won't"! They told me to take a risk, think positive, try.

Today, yesterday's objections are mere memories.

Thank You for showing me the light at the end of the tunnel. May I continue to walk in the light.

*"Man's ability is derived from God and does not
have to be acquired."*
                              James H. McReynolds

I woke this morning and remembered that
sobriety and serenity are gifts from God that
are freely given. I need only discover them
within my capacity to be honest. I need only
seek them in my new attitudes. I need only
discover them in the spiritual program for my
life.

God is alive in my life and His acceptance
of me is guaranteed.

*May I continue to discover more of Your beauty in
my life.*

*"When you see a snake, never mind where he
came from."*

W. G. Benham

So many alcoholics have died looking for
"the problem" that made them drink. The
wife, family, neighborhood or unemployment
was why they thought they got drunk. They
died seeking a reason. Alcoholics Anonymous
clearly states that alcohol is the problem for
alcoholics.

Alcohol *is* the problem! A statement that
is so simple yet so profound in its healing.
Today thousands upon thousands are choosing
not to die by not taking the first drink. To
see the problem clearly and honestly is the
beginning of wisdom. O.A., ACoA, N.A., G.A.,
Al-Anon and others have used these simple
principles with profound results. Do I see the
snake?

*Teach me to avoid those things that cause me pain
and destruction.*

"A man who thinks of himself as belonging to a particular national group in America has not yet become an American."

                        Woodrow Wilson

Today I know that I belong. I am not alone. I do not exist outside of the human race. I am an important part of this world.

Addiction makes us feel different, separated and isolated. It keeps us divided within ourselves, our family and relationships. So long as it can do this, it wins.

Now I know that I belong. I make up a part of the whole. Something of this universe is mine.

I am not an island unto myself. I am an essential part of the human race. I am at home in my world.

"We are looking in the wrong places for
happiness."
Robert J. McCracken

I sought happiness in the bottle. Others looked for "good feelings" in drugs, food or other people. Today I know that nothing that is outside of me can make me acceptable — acceptance must come from within.

I need to discover that spiritual place where I can be acceptable to me. Self-esteem is an essential part of my recovery and that can only be realized by making the spiritual journey within.

Today I seek to discover me. I want to know me —
because You created me.

"The worst sin towards our fellow creatures is not to hate them, but to be indifferent to them. That's the essence of inhumanity."
         George Bernard Shaw

For years I was indifferent to family and friends. And the tragedy was that because of my alcoholism I did not know it! For too long I was unaware of my disease and its multiple implications.

Today I am not indifferent. Spirituality teaches me that I am not a spectator but a participant. I am involved in my life and, ultimately, in the lives of others. Today I seek to practice the principles of sobriety in every area of my life. I not only seek to be sober on a daily basis, but I also seek to be honest, open and tolerant with other people.

The spiritual goal of sobriety and abstinence has placed me at the center of the universe and I know today that I make a difference to my fellow man.

Remove from me all attitudes of indifference and apathy. Make me a worthy steward in Your vineyard.

"There is no sort of work that could ever be done
well if you minded what fools say."
George Eliot

Part of the risk in my recovery is arousing
the displeasure of others. I know that I cannot
please all the people — and yet my disease tells
me that I must! For years I missed life's
opportunities because I listened to negative and
frightened people. Today I choose to shout my
"yes" to life, and I ignore the fools. The fools
are rarely friends. Rather, they seek to keep
me in the same prison as themselves. If they
truly loved me, they would encourage me to
be imaginative and creative.

Today I have a joyride "letting go and letting
God" because God is a great risk-taker!

I pray that I may always listen to the advice of
others, but never miss my power of decision.

*"Why would we kill off a good watchdog just
because he could not fly?"*

Frank Mar

God has created this world with variety and
we all have different gifts. Some people make
music, others write stories and many are
practical at home or in industry. We need to
understand what gifts and skills we have and
develop them.

It is both fruitless and negative to spend our
time complaining that we are not like other
people — or are without their talents. Such
an attitude stops us from discovering our own
creative talents. We are so busy comparing
ourselves with others that we miss our own
uniqueness.

Today I enjoy discovering more about me
and the abundant gifts that God has freely
given to me. What about you?

*I pray that I may be truly grateful for what
I have.*

*"Your temper is the only thing that doesn't get
better with age."*

Anonymous

I lost my temper when I was in the wrong
and wanted to protect myself. My temper was
closely associated with my ego and pride; I
hated to admit I was in the wrong.

Today I know that I am not God. I make
mistakes and apologize. I don't have to have
an answer. It is okay to be imperfect and
human. And you know what I am finding? I
don't lose my temper so much!

*I pray that I may express my anger and discomfort
without having a selfish temper tantrum.*

*"Nobody in this world is more secure than a man
in a penitentiary."*
                   Harvey S. Firestone, Jr.

In one sense it is safe to live in a prison
— but at what price? To live is to be free and
have the responsibility of choice. Addiction
removes this freedom of choice; addiction takes
away our freedom.

In sobriety I am involved in the joys of risk.
I experience the pleasure and pain that comes
with the responsibility of choice. Today I know
I am living — yesterday I had to read about
it!

*God, I thank You for the confusing gift
of freedom.*

*"I have never doubted that God created man for
great purposes . . ."*
                    Preston Bradley

I am special today. I know that there is a
purpose for my life and that it is essentially
good and creative. I know that beauty is not
just in things that I can see . . . beauty is also
in me. Today I affirm my great purpose in this
world . . . to be the best that I can be.

For too many years I gave my God-given
power away; I gave it to alcohol, I gave it to
people, I gave it to a belief system that did
not make sense to me. Today I am discovering
the power that God has given to me, and I
feel good about myself. Today I reclaim my
divinity.

*Creator of this wonderful universe, make me an
instrument of Your peace.*

*"A man never discloses his own character so
clearly as when he describes another's."*
                                    Johann Paul Richter

I was always so perceptive when it came to
assessing the character faults of others. I could
offer the best therapy and treatment to others;
the best advice in the world. I was excellent
at "pulling the covers" on a con-man — but
always I missed me! I never really heard my
insights. I never followed my advice. I always
minimized my character faults.

Usually what I saw in others was reflected
in my own personality. The things I loathed
in others existed in me. The anger and resentments came from a denial of self.

In sobriety I hear the advice of others. I don't
always like it but I hear it. I give criticism and
today I am growing in my acceptance of
criticism.

*In relationships may I see clearly my own
reflection.*

*"The university exists only to find and
communicate the truth."*
Robert Maynard Hutchins

Today in my recovery I know I am a student
of Truth and will hopefully be so until the day
that I die. No longer do I search for the cheap
thrill or the quick fix — now I desire lasting
truths.

Spirituality is about finding God in things
that are true and honest, good and wholesome,
creative and positive.

I battle daily with that sick side of me that
is greedy, selfish and dishonest — I'm not
perfect. Today I know that the sick and
dishonest way of living does not work. My
history teaches me that it does not work. I was
never truly happy knowing that the gains came
at the expense of others. Now I am a student
in the "university of life", and I enjoy learning
something new about me every day. Today I
am able to listen — listen to those who are
wiser than I. I know that I do not have all
the answers — and with this knowledge comes
freedom.

*God, who lives in and through Truth, continue to
radiate and illuminate my life.*

> *"If other people are going to talk, conversation*
> *becomes impossible."*
> *James McNeill Whistler*

Part of my addiction was never listening to what people were saying. This was part arrogance, part denial, part fear, part control, part ego — the bottom line was that I did not listen. I was bored and unhappy with my life because I was a prisoner of my own thoughts.

My spiritual awakening — which I consider a process rather than an event, a process that is still going on in my life on a daily basis — was in allowing some new information into my life that led to admittance and acceptance. The day that I was able to admit that I was an alcoholic was the day I took a step towards acceptance.

Today I receive immense help and comfort from other people, especially recovering alcoholics. Two people experiencing an honest conversation are part of God's promised love for His world.

Let the words I hear be acceptable in Your sight.

"Style is the man himself."
Georges Louis Leclerc de Buffon

Style is involved in Spirituality — especially when it concerns the recovering addict. Sobriety and serenity are not just seen in what we say or do or in our ability to keep away from the first drink or pill — they are seen in our creative styles. How we feel about ourselves should be seen in the confidence of our gait and the concern for personal appearance. Personal hygiene is important because it reflects a love of self. Physical health and exercise reveal a desire and interest in life, fitness and energy.

Style may not make the man but it certainly reveals the man!

May I seek to reveal the beauty You gave me with my appearance and style.

*Treat people
as if
they were
what they
ought to be,
and you help
them to become
what they are
capable
of being.*

Goethe

*"Optimism is a kind of heart stimulant — the
digitalis of failure."*
                                        Elbert Hubbard

Today I am an optimist. I believe in life, and
more importantly, I believe in me. I know that
God cares and this brings me hope.

But when I was drinking I had a negative
and destructive attitude in all areas of life;
nothing pleased me, people were not to be
trusted, everybody had a price, God seemed to
be "out for lunch" and life had lost its meaning.
I was a sad man. I was a lonely man. I was
an angry man.

When I was told to put down the drink and
follow some new directions, I halfheartedly
agreed. I met people who laughed, shared their
pain and lived in the realistic "now". I began
to listen. Slowly I changed. Peace was within
my grasp.

Today I wonder at my halfhearted risk that
started it all — and thank God.

*Teach me to look beyond the shadows to the
sun's rays.*

"Every man's memory is his private literature."
                                        Aldous Huxley

What it was like. What happened. What it is like today. Memory. If I am to stay sober, I need to remember. I need to remember on a daily basis. I must never forget.

My life is reflected in my memory. The "writing on the wall" is really in my head, but am I prepared to see it and acknowledge it? For years I chose not to remember. I lived in a world of make-believe. People were exaggerating the facts! With denial at the center of my life I was able to forget the pain and drink again, only to awake to yesterday's pain again.

My memory is the key to my recovery. Spirituality is about "seeing" — seeing my life as it is, rather than how I imagined or hoped it would be. My pain belongs in my life because it is mine! Alcohol always works; but does it work for me or against me? My remembering helps me answer that question today and hopefully tomorrow.

Thank You, God, for allowing my yesterdays to forge my tomorrows.

"One of the greatest necessities in America is to discover creative solitude."
                    Carl Sandburg

I need to be alone. Being alone is not the same as being lonely. I need to be alone with me in order to love me, understand me, hear my needs and plan my day.

Also solitude is a spiritual experience because it enables me to center on what God is doing and creating in my life. Solitude enables me to think and cooperate with His will for me in our world.

As an addict I was always running around being "busy". Today I rest within myself in order to be more active and creative.

Let me be still so that I can enjoy my world.

*"Humility is to make a right estimate of
one's self."*
              Charles Haddon Spurgeon

To see yourself as a good person is part of the program of humility. To see your gifts and recognize your achievements is what it is to be a humble person. "God does not make junk." Therefore, we should not act or behave towards ourselves in a way that would indicate anything other than that we are "special".

All addicts and alcoholics need to accept this because for years we had felt guilty, lonely and ashamed. These attitudes helped to keep us sick.

Sobriety and serenity is recognizing our God-given uniqueness that makes us "special". We can achieve great things as long as we continue to believe in ourselves.

*Thank You for loving me enough to become a part
of me.*

"All are but parts of one stupendous whole.
Whose body nature is, and God the soul."
                                    Alexander Pope

I belong to this world, this mighty universe — but more importantly, it belongs to me. I have a responsibility in this world and to this world. No longer can I abrogate my responsibility. God created and is creating through me. What I say, what I do, how I feel is important. I am important. I am terrific — because God made me and works through me.

Sometimes I feel the one-ness. I stand on a mountain top and look at the rolling hills beyond and I feel noble. The birds sing, the streams murmur and I feel a tremendous sense of joy.

But I also feel the pain of the world. The people suffering, the pointlessness of man's violence and the injustice of prejudice. All this I feel, too.

Spirituality involves this mixture, the paradox of my being an angel in the dust!

Thank You for including me in Your design for
life. I tremble at the responsibility You have
shared with me.

"The only thing we have to fear is fear itself."
                          Franklin Delano Roosevelt

Fear is a killer. It is a killer because it drains us of life, energy and creativity. Fear petrifies the human spirit.

I spent a lot of yesterdays afraid. Afraid of people finding out. Afraid of the telephone. Afraid of where it would all end. Afraid of me! I did not realize that I was feeding the fear with my behavior. I drank myself into fear. The day I stopped drinking alcohol was the day I stopped giving energy to my fear.

Today I live my life without abnormal or unrealistic fears. Today I enjoy my life. I work through my problems. I am not afraid of my shadow. Today I love me.

Lord may I always connect my unrealistic fears with my behavior — and begin the change.

"Without work all life goes rotten."
                              Albert Camus

A spiritual discovery that I have made is that I work in order to be, not simply to exist. To work is human. Work opens the door to the meaning of life, and it stops life from being boring and dull. Work is creative. When I was drinking, I did not have this understanding of work and so it became a burden, something I had to get through, something I had to do for money or security. I missed the creative dynamic of work and how it could enable me to feel good about myself.

In recovery I work, create and grow not only in my job, but also in my leisure hours. Indeed the distinction between the two often overlaps because the program I take into the office is the same program I take into the party or disco. Today God is to be found in everything.

In the many aspects of my work I am made to feel alive.

"A liar needs a good memory."
          Quintilian

I lied to impress. I lied to hide my guilt and shame. I lied to cover my mistakes. I lied to bridge the silence. I lied to fantasize. I lied to hurt and destroy. I lied to hide the real me. Then I lied to cover the lies. Then I lied to cover the lies I told to cover the original lies! So it went on. Endless. Exhausting. Meaningless. A part of me always loathed the lies I told. Then I grew to hate myself.

Today, because I understand spirituality to be based on truth, I try not to tell lies. When I do lie, I make an effort to correct myself and apologize. Today lying is painful for me. Today I try to use my mind, imagination and memory for better things.

O God, who gave mankind the miracle of language and communication, let me not abuse Your gift with destructive deceit.

"Science without religion is lame, religion without science is blind."
Albert Einstein

In the field of addiction we need to work together and listen to the professionalism we all bring: the answer will be in "the many".

So often we divide ourselves up into "ghettos" of learning and miss what "the others" are saying — and the disease wins! This is reminiscent of the old days in the church when science was seen as the enemy, the world was flat and the earth was the center of the universe. Pride and ego kept people sick, isolated and afraid — and thousands suffered and died. However, people began to listen to each other and the world benefited from the shared wisdom.

As addictionologists and recovering people we need to listen to each other.

Help me to see You in the honest experience of every man.

*"The good neighbor looks beyond the external
accidents and discerns those inner qualities
that make all men human and,
therefore, brothers."*
                                    Martin Luther King, Jr.

As a drunk I said cruel things about other
people. My prejudices hid my fears and insecurities. I condemned in others what I saw in
myself. I deflected attention from me by the
name-calling of others: sick manipulations.
"Neighbor" was only a word that I could spell
and interpret, useful for religious homilies or
pretentious innuendos but not something I
really experienced.

Today I am able to be the "good neighbor"
to many people, known and unknown. My
recovery has brought people into my life.
Relationships mean something; friends are
important; the world is one. Black, Asian,
Hispanic — all add a variety to my life that
enable me to get in touch with buried feelings
of my "difference". In the stranger I discover
something of myself; the foreigner has become
both friend and neighbor.

*God, I never cease to be amazed at the mystery and
variety that is "me".*

*"To be able to be caught up in a world of thought
— that is being educated."*
                    Edith Hamilton

For years I didn't think I reacted. Things happened and I felt I had to respond — but rarely was it a considered response. I had no program for my life. I was like a boat without a sail.

Today I think before I speak. I talk things over with a sponsor or friends before I make an important decision. I listen to the opinions of others before I make a choice. Today I am caught up in a world of thought and it isn't simply my own. God knows my best thinking nearly killed me!

The world only makes sense because people share. It is the giving and receiving that makes life worthwhile. To be an island unto myself is isolation. I know what it was to be lonely. Today I desire a relationship of mind, body and feelings.

*Let me find You in my neighbor and be sustained
by the stranger.*

"To love oneself is the beginning of a life-long romance."

Oscar Wilde

Today I am able to say that I love myself. To love myself is to love God and the world in which I live. I cannot befriend, hug, help or create without first having a relationship with myself. Without me, there is no meaning to my life. I am the most important thing in my life. This is not said to be conceited but is an aspect of self-love. It reveals a healthy pride and respect for my life. And it feels good.

For years I thought that to love "self" was wrong and sinful, a misuse of energy and time. What people thought about me was so important; what people said about me was a constant worry. And the more I looked out of myself for meaning, the more lost, isolated and confused I became. Then I heard that God loved me and He wanted me to love me. Today I live and love through me.

O God who created me to love, let me begin with me.

"The greatest good of a minority of our generation may be the greatest good for the greatest number of people in the long run."
        Oliver Wendell Holmes, Jr.

I belong to a minority. I am a recovering alcoholic. I use a spiritual program that keeps me sober a day at a time. I have a God that I can understand today. I do a daily inventory and make amends when appropriate, and I feel good about myself.

This spiritual program is reaching out to the world: gamblers, overeaters, cocaine addicts, the families of addicts, the children of compulsive people; obsessive people can all be helped by this daily program of acceptance.

Perhaps the recovering drunk has stumbled upon a miracle that can bring the world back to God!

Lord, the more I talk about my "difference" with people, the more they and I feel the same.

*"Middle-age is when you begin to smile at things
that used to cause you to laugh."*

Anonymous

Today I feel so young at heart. I love to
laugh, I mean really laugh; I love to play and
act silly in my life; I love discovering my "child"
that comes out to give balance to my life.

This was not always the case. Not too many
yesterdays ago I was serious, depressed, affecting
a smile that did not come from within. Alcoholism made me an unhappy man. Before I
got sober my so called "high" had changed into
a boring "low"!

I was middle-aged before I was thirty. Today
I feel younger than I did twenty years ago —
and it shows. You are what you drink. Today
I am sober!

Thank You for the gift of "play" in my life.

*"We find it hard to believe that other people's
thoughts are as silly as our own, but they
probably are."*
James Harvey Robinson

Today I am able to laugh at myself. I even
"think" funny things. I sit at airports and look
at the faces, postures and mannerisms of the
people passing by and I smile, giggle and laugh
in my handkerchief. Then I think about what
a funny man I am — so ridiculously proud,
so pompous about the silliest things, so preoccupied about my own importance — and it
is funny.

Yes, today I am able to laugh at myself. I
know that people are funny because I know
I am. At meetings I hear people laughing about
the day's insanities and I can always identify.
Even my relationships are humorous. I try so
hard to make a good impression while at the
same time offering the effect of detachment
— trying to be "cool".

God must have a sense of humor because
He made you and me!

*Thank You for the gift of humor — it allows true
humility to develop.*

"The worst vice of the fanatic is his sincerity."
                                    Oscar Wilde

The disease of alcoholism is "cunning, baffling and powerful", and it manipulates us to believe "the lie". There is a point that we reach in our disease where we believe that crazy behavior is acceptable. Insanity becomes the order of the day. And when friends or therapists try to give us a message, we discount them.

How can we break down this wall of denial? Well, there is strength in numbers. If everybody we respect is disagreeing with us, then it is time that we change. If our isolation has become a source of martyrdom, then we need to reorganize our attitude for living. Insanity and isolation are often companions; they feed off each other.

We need always to stay close to our recovering community. Strength and sobriety is in numbers.

God, You gave me the message to become the message. Help me to live it in the recovering community.

"I cannot give you the formula for success, but I can give you the formula for failure, which is try to please everybody."
                                    Herbert Bayard Swope

Part of my recovery is not that I never "people-please" but that I know when I am doing it . . . and I am doing it less!

My low self-esteem was revealed in the way I would say what I felt you wanted to hear, do what you wanted to do, go where you wanted to go — and for years I missed me. For years I missed my life because I was preoccupied with other people. And I wasn't honest. I hated being that way but I wouldn't admit it. Now I see that my guilt around my addiction led me into this sick cycle, and recovery is taking me out of it. Today I say "I don't want to go." "I don't agree with what you are saying." "I refuse to do that."

My dignity is being discovered in my straight forwardness.

God, may I have the courage to share my true feelings.

*"A fanatic is one who can't change his mind and
won't change the subject."*
                          Winston Churchill

In my addiction I had a closed mind because
I was afraid to be seen to be wrong. I had to
be right, I had to be in control, and I had to
be perfect. To say "I don't know the answer"
would make me weak, vulnerable and human!
So I developed a closed mind: my way, my
thoughts, my ideas, my life, my God. And I
was in pain.

Then I had a moment of clarity. I heard that
I was sick. I heard that if I really wanted help,
I could receive it. I put away the alcohol and
I became vulnerable. Slowly I faced the con-
fusion of life and I discovered the human race.
I was no longer alone.

Today the spiritual life is more about living
with the questions than providing the answers.

*I pray that I may continue to find Truth in
variety.*

"Often the test of courage is not to die but to live."
Conte Vittorio Alfieri

There are many ways of committing suicide. The obvious way is to take your life — the ultimate escape. One can reach that point in life when there seems no hope, no purpose in living and death is attractive. Many alcoholics and addicts reach this point of despair.

However, there is a more subtle way of "suicide", which is to kill yourself slowly — by a sick behavior and a negative attitude. I was "dying" in a lifestyle that revolved around alcohol. All I wanted to do was drink — I didn't want to go anywhere, be with anyone or enjoy the thousand and one pleasures that life offers. I was dying in my life. I was becoming a "walking zombie". I was committing suicide by degrees!

Today I can see this and I am glad I had the courage to live. My act of courage began with my "no" to alcohol.

Let me continue to live in my life.

"The mass of men lead lives of quiet desperation."
                         Henry David Thoreau

I thought that I was the only one who felt
like I did. Nobody could possibly understand.
I was different from everybody and needed to
keep my life — my true life — a secret. I was
living a life of quiet desperation! Then I went
to a meeting for recovering alcoholics and
heard somebody share my pain, my loneliness,
my confusion, my addiction — my life.

I was lonely because I kept myself separate
from people. I saw them as being different from
myself, and so I remained the lonely and
isolated victim. Strange how similar we are
when we begin to share. When we get beneath
culture, class and creed, we discover sensitive
human beings trying to make sense of their
lives. We need each other.

*May I risk rejection in my spiritual need to share
and be known.*

*"I shall pass through this world but once. If,
therefore, there be any kindness I can show, or any
good thing I can do, let me do it now; let me not
defer it or neglect it, for I shall not
pass this way again."*
                                        Etienne de Grellet

Today I know that God requires me to be
involved in my recovery and sobriety. God has
always wanted me to be sober but the miracle
took place when I wanted it, too. His hands
were always extended towards me, the miracle
happened when I chose to embrace Him. My
sobriety involves me.

Today I understand that sobriety is more
than "not picking up the first drink"; it
involves quiet acts of kindness to myself and
others. God works through me — through my
hands, my smile, my voice, my love and my
acceptance. When an opportunity arises for me
to be ordinarily kind, I intend to give it; God
knows I have needed such kindnesses from
others in the past.

*May I never avoid an opportunity for shared
healing.*

> *"If you're not allowed to laugh in heaven, I don't*
> *want to go there."*
>
> *Martin Luther*

When I was a practicing alcoholic, I imagined heaven to be a dull formal place, rather like a never-ending cathedral. Beautiful, but serious. My pain and guilt were so great that I rarely laughed, and when I did it was usually inappropriate and violent: I laughed at others!

Today heaven is associated with recovery. It is a place of joy, acceptance and forgiveness. A place where people can be themselves and where variety abounds. Christians play with people from other religions — and the atheists make the music! The laughter of "peace" abounds. I am "at one" with my Father and all my brothers and sisters. I am home!

God of Love, when I hear the sound of laughter
here on earth, I think what joy awaits me in
heaven.

"Take away love and our earth is a tomb."
Robert Browning

Spirituality is essentially love. It is the love that suffers and grows in the acceptance of my compulsive and obsessive behavior. It is the love that requires a knowledge of "self" in order to give understanding and respect to others. Spirituality is that loving vulnerability that creates healing in recovery. It provides meaning to life and relationships.

The world is a creative place, and we will only find happiness when we begin to create. God has created us to take and make — give and receive. With the suffering, loneliness, struggle and acceptance comes a love that is real and alive.

Teach me to live in my life
and not merely exist.

"God is not a cosmic bellboy."
Harry Emerson Fosdick

My understanding of God is within the context of freedom. God is involved in His world but He allows it an autonomy. We are not puppets on a string. When things begin to go wrong, God does not interfere and make changes (usually) without our cooperation. God reveals the extent of His love by allowing us a creative responsibility in our lives.

For years I did not understand this. I thought that if I prayed enough, He would answer all my prayers and come to my rescue. When He didn't, I grew confused, angry and resentful. What was I doing wrong? Where was God in my life? He didn't love me. Why wasn't God my cosmic co-dependent?

Today I love His detachment. Today I grow in my freedom. Today I cooperate with His miracle.

Lord, thank You for allowing me the freedom
to fail.

*"Prayer is not asking. It is a language of
the soul."*
                    Mohandas Gandhi

At school I was told that prayer is "talking
to God". Then I discovered that prayer is more
than this — prayer is a relationship with God.
It is a two-way system — I talk to God but
I must also listen to Him. Like any relationship
that is going to work and grow, it needs time.
I must spend time developing my relationship
with God. I must create an awareness of His
presence in my life because I believe He is
always there for me.

But more than this, prayer is a yearning for
truth within the center of my being. In prayer
I get in touch with that part of me that will
be forever restless until it finds rest, eternal
rest, in Him.

O God, prayer is my journey into You.

*"You can't hold a man down without staying
down with him."*
                                        Booker T. Washington

I know who was holding me down in my life.
I was. I know who was bringing pain and sadness
in my life. I was. I know who was making me
the victim of addiction. I was. I would beat
myself up and then complain about the bruises!

I did this because I could not "see". I had
not accepted or understood the implications
of my alcoholism. Today I am beginning to take
care of myself because I have accepted my
disease. I do not choose today to be the enemy
in my life — I have surrendered to live. I do
not want to hurt anymore. I do not want to
hide in guilt and fear anymore. I do not choose
to be my victim today.

*God, I thank You for the freedom to determine my
life and my victories.*

"Do not mistake activity for achievement."
                                    Mabel Newcomber

Often I am running in circles and not getting anywhere. I spend forever "doing" things and yet I know I am not achieving anything. I am going nowhere in my life!

"Be still and know that I am God." I need to stop. I need to listen to the pain that is within. I need to relax in my gratitude. I need to rest in myself. Tomorrow has not yet come — today I take time for me.

Lord, I hear Your still small voice. Today I rest in
me and discover Thee.

*"Good people are good because they've come to
wisdom through failure."*
                    William Saroyan

Today I am able to learn from my mistakes
because I can see that they really were mistakes! I was trying to play the game of life
without a full deck. My big mistake in life was
trying to drink alcohol like a non-alcoholic. I
couldn't do it.

Drugs do not think; they react. They always
work, and for me they worked against me. Most
of my failures in life stemmed from a funda-
mental misconception — alcoholics cannot
drink like non-alcoholics! This I now accept.
And in a strange way that is difficult to explain,
I am a stronger person for having lived through
my alcoholism. God has become more real, the
world is more comprehensible, my life is more
understandable because of the pain.

If a part of "goodness" is knowing that you
are not perfect, then on a daily basis I am
becoming a good person.

*God, who has created a world in which there is
pain and failure, help me to accept both as vehicles
to wisdom.*

*"It is human nature to think wisely and act
foolishly."*
                                            Anatole France

I experienced blackouts in my drinking.
Often I would wake up and not know where
I had been, what I had said or what I had done.
I would awake to peer through windows
searching for my car. I would telephone to find
out what time I had left the party and if
anything had happened. Often as I bathed I
would discover bruises or bleeding from an
unremembered incident.

There were other times I knew what I had
done, knew what I had said, remembered how
I behaved — and yet still I went back for more.
I drank alcoholically for years because my pride
would not allow me to be alcoholic. I created
the wisest excuses for staying sick!

Today my sobriety requires a wisdom that
is based on reality.

*Lord of action, teach me to place my feet alongside
my best thinking.*

"Prayer of the modern American: 'Dear God, I pray for patience. And I want it right now!' "
                                    Oren Arnold

How I appreciate those times when I experience the gift of patience in my life, not as often as I would like. That is an interesting point: I am impatient about having patience!

Seriously, patience is when I recognize the need to "back off" — allow God into the driver's seat, resting in the knowledge that things happen in God's time. This does not mean that I am not involved, but it allows for God's comprehensive plan for His world. I can experience patience usually when I get in touch with gratitude. Once I stop giving energy to the "I wants", the joy of serenity breathes through my life and I can rest. Sometimes I need to "stop" and say a loud and resonant "thank you".

Lord, let me breathe these words into my life:
"Thy will be done."

> *"We are all here for a spell, get all the good*
> *laughs you can."*
>
> Will Rogers

When I first heard recovering alcoholics
laughing, I thought I was in the wrong place.
I was angry that they treated the disease so
lightly. Then slowly I began to see that laughter
is part of joy — a deep joy that comes from
personal healing. Laughter is spiritual because
it is a positive response to life. It is the noise
of optimism.

And there is so much in life to laugh about
— not only the funny things we did, but also
the "humor" that abounds in living. How
funny is our self-righteousnes! How amusing we
are in courtship. How ridiculous we appear
when we pretend to be serious and "in charge".

Laughter is the conversation of angels.

Let me see the miracle of humor in the gift of life
— and let me be prepared to share it.

*"The books that the world calls immoral are the
books that show the world its own shame."*
                                        Oscar Wilde

In my addiction I avoided things that I did
not like, did not want to face, did not want
to consider. I hid from life and condemned
things I did not wish to understand. My ego
created a hypocritical purity that enabled me
to judge, condemn and abuse the thoughts and
ideas of those I considered inferior to myself.

Today I try to live and let live. I do this
not to avoid conflict or criticism but because
I have found, through experience, how my
ideas and attitudes have changed during my
years of recovery. People who I would have
condemned to Hell have now become my
friends and mentors. Concepts and lifestyles
that were once abhorrent to me are now
appreciated and inspiring. What was once
dismissed as immoral is today, for me, a part
of life.

*God of Truth and Reality, help me to accept the
difference that is in others.*

"Freedom is not enough."
                    Lyndon B. Johnson

The gift of freedom requires the acknowledgement of the benefactor, God. To experience freedom without realizing its source is to miss the point; freedom requires responsibility.

When I was drinking, I demanded freedom without responsibility and I suffered. I created in freedom my own horror stories. I hurt others because I did not respect in them what I demanded for myself and slowly, ever so slowly, freedom slipped away.

Today I believe that my spiritual program reinforces my responsibility for my life. God has created me with free will and I need to respect this gift in others. If I do not respect others, I will never receive it. Dignity is a two way street.

Thank You for the freedom to experience myself in my treatment of my neighbor.

"I am not afraid of tomorrow, for I have seen
yesterday and I love today."
William Allen White

Today I have confidence in my life and I am experiencing consistency in my behavior and attitude. In recovery, things follow a natural progression and life is more like a series of curves than sharp peaks. As an addict, my life was forever going up and down, ecstasy followed by gloom; the "best ever" followed by depression; always black and white — no grays.

Today I have some balance and consistency. Things are connected and grow in the process of change. Sudden happenings and quick changes scare me because they are symptomatic of yesterday's disease and are not consistent with the spiritual life I seek. Today I have the peace of knowing that tomorrow will be something like today — and I am happy.

Thank You for the spiritual gift of consistency.

"The books I haven't written are better than the books other people have."
Cyril V. Connolly

Today I still have to grapple with pride, vanity and conceit. Today, thanks to God and my spiritual program, I am not so preoccupied with self, but the old tapes can still be heard: "Thank God I am not as stupid as her." "I am blessed in not being like those people." "I suppose everybody in the room is looking at me."

Pride is still a big obstacle because it keeps me isolated from people. It emphasizes the difference between me and the world, rather than the commonality. Pride keeps me a prisoner of my ego and develops that cruel and sadistic streak in my nature that I know exists. Pride stops me being grateful because it keeps me too focused on what I am doing and I miss the beauty and splendor of my life. Pride keeps my nose pushed against the picture so I cannot see the portrait!

I can only change this "proudful" attitude by talking about it. The way for me to grow is to "dump it" . . . today.

May I find me in the people I meet and share with.

"Forgiveness is the key to action and freedom."
Hannah Arendt

Early in sobriety I found it easy to forgive others but hard to forgive myself. This kept me sick and negative, even in recovery, because I was unable to practice self-love. I still blamed me and felt responsible for being alcoholic. I had not surrendered to the reality of alcoholism as a disease.

Then a moment of sanity was granted me whereby I understood that I was not responsible for being alcoholic, but that I am responsible for my recovery. And my recovery involves a love and respect of self. This knowledge brought a tremendous joy and freedom that led to action within the recovering community. Only by loving me will I be able to love you, and in both these ways I show my love of God.

May I always hold on to the spiritual power
of forgiveness.

"The first and great commandment is 'Don't let them scare you.'"

Elmer Davis

In my sobriety I still need to deal with fear. A fear of people, a fear of not being good enough, a fear of saying the wrong thing, a fear of not looking "good enough" — fear still haunts me in sobriety.

However, my recovery also tells me that I am a child of God. I am a beautiful and powerful human being because God not only made me, but has shared something of His precious divinity with me. I am good enough. In Him I can afford to risk. Love must begin with the recognition of self.

Today I must remember that people are not "out to get me". I need not make myself the victim. People are much the same inside, and we all need each other to survive.

Thank You for the power to live with my fear.

*"Intelligence is proved not by ease of learning but
by understanding what we learn."*
                                    Joseph Whitney

For years I learned things without understanding what the words, or the meaning
behind the words, really meant. An example
was alcoholism. Then a man said, "My name
is Bill, and I am an alcoholic and a recovering
human being!" Then it struck me; recovery
from a drug — alcohol — was not simply about
putting down the glass but about changing and
developing a positive lifestyle as a human being.

The same is true with spirituality. It is not
about being religious, going to church or
accepting dogma. It is about finding God in
my life, discovering God in the decisions and
actions I take and seeing Him in the world
around me. Today I understand spirituality to
be the link that unites all peoples and is
centered on what is true and real.

*May I continue to search for the meaning within
the word and the harmony of communication.*

*"I believe the first test of a really great man
is humility."*

John Ruskin

An understanding of humility that makes
sense to me is that of the man who is aware
of his limitations but still reaches for the stars.

For years I thought that humility was
groveling in the dirt. Keeping quiet and acting
obsequious. Being a religious doormat for
others to walk upon.

Nothing could be further from the truth!
Humility is about speaking your mind, fighting
for your ideas and opinions, creating through
effort, sweat and debate. The humble man's
ego is based on reality — not fed on illusion.
When he is wrong, he can admit it and is open
to the ideas of others.

Humility is based upon a realistic self-love.

*O God, let me humbly rejoice in Your gift
of creativity.*

*"Art, if it is to be reckoned with as one of the
great values of life, must teach
men . . . tolerance."*
Somerset Maugham

There is something about art that is accepting, tolerant and reconcilable with "difference". I have observed that artists — those
who paint, write, dance, sculpture, design —
are also people who are accepting and tolerant
because they need the "different" in order to
create and progress. Things cannot stay the
same and art is the recorder of man's journey
towards the truth; but mankind needs friction,
argument, confrontation, rejection — yes,
"difference" in order to grow and develop.

People say that artists are crazy, and I
suppose this is true. But we need crazy people
to take the world where it needs to go. In the
crazy, the seed of genius is often buried.

*Lord, before I reject the artist or the "crazy", let
me seriously consider the message.*

"Art is not a thing; it is a way."
                                      Elbert Hubbard

In the spiritual twelve-step program it talks about ". . . a God as you understand Him." This is a liberating concept that teaches us to risk and think "big". God is not only found in churches, temples and rituals — God can be found in the myriad of art forms. God is always to be found in the creative. Because art is always concerned with life and truth, God is always involved.

Today I am able to look for God in His or Her World.

In my recovery from the disease of addiction I need to discover the wonder and splendor of life that got damaged in my drinking days. Art can help me to feel again. It helps me to think and be concerned again. Art teaches me to be involved in life.

Thank You for the artist — another aspect
            of priesthood.

"I invent nothing. I rediscover."
Auguste Rodin

I believe that spirituality is given to every human being and we need only discover it in our lives to experience its power. The history of my life has been more of a "cycle" than a straight line leading into the distance. I am constantly returning to past events, reminiscences and experiences that were part of my yesterdays but converge into my present. I am rediscovering my yesterdays in my todays; the fruits of my tomorrows are planted within today.

So it seems that my journey is not simply forward. It also involves a rediscovery of yesterday in today. My life is a mystery that exists within God.

O Lord, with You eternity is ever present and occasionally I get a glimpse of it.

> *"I am the inferior of any man whose rights I*
> *trample underfoot."*
>
> Horace Greeley

Now I can see my feelings of inferiority in the assumed arrogance of my past behavior. Now I see that behind the pride was the need to prove myself. The manipulation was a cover for my insecurity.

At some point years ago I accepted the idea that I was not good enough and needed to pretend to be something different. The use of alcohol was part of this disease process. Money, friends, fast cars and debts were all drawn into the delusion.

Today I am learning to accept me. I am not a millionaire, I will probably never be a millionaire and so I do not need to adopt the lifestyle of a millionaire! I work in an office. I drive a Ford. But today I am happy. Today I can pay my bills. Today I have friends who are involved in my life. Today I do not have to put people down to feel important. Today I have discovered that the people I treated with disdain are just like me.

I pray that I may receive healing and forgiveness
from those I considered inferior.

*"I am one individual on a small planet in a little
solar system in one of the galaxies."*
                                        Roberto Assagioli

Spirituality develops a humility that is
realistic. Realism teaches me that I am one
among many. That does not mean that I am
less than anybody else, but it certainly doesn't
mean that I am above others.

Arrogance, fantasy and selfishness are characteristics of addiction that stop the development of true individuality. To pretend to be
something we are not, or have a grandiose
illusion about our own importance, misses the
truth, misses our truth and misses our individuality.

Humility is treating people with the respect
we would want, giving people the freedom we
require in our life. Humility is perceiving our
God-given talent and individuality.

*I pray that I will remember that I am a "part of",
rather than the sum total of this universe.*

"One man with courage is a majority."
                                    Thomas Jefferson

Alcoholism made me afraid of my shadow. I became so petrified with fear that I could not enjoy my life. And I felt that I could do nothing. My disease told me I was helpless. I existed in an atmosphere of doom and gloom.

Then I experienced a "moment" of sanity when I saw that I was the problem in my life. My pain was being caused by my actions and attitudes. I took courage, confronted the disease in my life and decided to take small steps towards recovery. I have built my confidence on that "moment" of courage I took years ago. I am not an island unto myself. I am not alone. God is with me in my life.

Teach me to have the courage to be what You have created. May I accept my miracle.

"The great law of culture: let each become all that he was created capable of being."
                                        Thomas Carlyle

We are capable of great things. This history of man, although surrounded by wars and unspeakable acts of violence, is also the history of art, music, poetry and romance. Each person is capable of great and noble acts — but do we want to do them? We can be honest, loving and caring people only if we choose to be that. The power of freedom and choice is the determining factor in all our lives. Each culture has imaginative and creative features, but it is the people that make them happen. Nothing will happen unless people decide to make it happen.

So it is with the culture of recovery. The people who make up the recovering community in all the addictions are the people who made a decision and acted upon it. Talk is cheap and cruel unless it is followed by an event. Decisions must be made real. We all have the capacity to be honest and kind.

May I not only be grateful for my culture but may I live to add something to it.

"You've got to be a fool to want to stop the march of time."

Pierre Renoir

My fear of the future gave me a fear of change. My need to "control" made me avoid any new or confusing ideas. My alcoholism wanted me to escape and hide in the past — tomorrow was too fearful to be contemplated. At other times — and this is why alcoholism is cunning, baffling and powerful — I would want to escape into tomorrow and avoid the reality of today.

Time and reality were to be "played with" rather than experienced. But time moves on, it progresses just like the disease, and if I am to be a winner in this world, I need to move with it. God is to be experienced in the "march of time" and today I want to be in a relationship with Him.

Teach me to respect time as an opportunity for growth.

*"Our concern is not how to worship in the
catacombs but how to remain human in
the skyscrapers."*

Abraham Heschel

Worship requires the discovery of "true
worth" in my own life. True worship is not
only historical and traditional but also contem-
porary. I need to discover not only the God
of yesterday, but also the God of the modern
city.

My past addiction to fantasy often made me
place God in an unreal world. I was happy
talking about the Jews, Romans and Philistines
but I missed God in Las Vegas, on freeways
and in local politics.

God is alive in His world, and it is tragic
to make Him a prisoner of history.

Let me find You in the place where I live.

*"Tact is the art of making a point without making
an enemy."*
Howard W. Newton

An aspect of my recovery is not hurting
people's feelings unnecessarily. I am learning
how to say what I have to say without causing
offense. Today I am learning to be tactful and
respectful.

As a drunk I would say the first thing that
came into my head without any regard for the
feelings of others. I was often violent with
words, sarcastic with comments and cruel in
dialogue. Tact was a sign of weakness; gentleness and sensitivity were unmanly; my power
was seen in forcing people to change their
minds!

Today I do not wish to be like this. Today
I desire to be tactful.

*Lord, let me always express my opinion
respectfully.*

*"The older I grow, the more I listen to people who
don't say much."*
                                Germain G. Glidden

I've noticed that an important part of my
recovery is people-watching. I have fun watching people — at a party, on a train or in a
park. I find the daily "theater" of life fascinating and stimulating. I also learn so much
about me by observing others. I can identify
with their mannerisms, actions and facial antics
and intuitively sense what they are feeling. I
see their fear, hesitancy and shame and connect
it with mine. People are a mirror to my life.

Part of my recovery is developing that
instinctive spirituality that grows through
observation. The human being is forever
communicating, sending energy and messages
not only with words but by his existence —
and especially by his silence. Sometimes a
person's silence can be deafening! God is most
alive to me in the lives and behavior of His
people, and part of my worship and prayer is
observing the splendor and richness of my
fellow human beings.

*You, who have created the universe in such
magnificent silence, touch me with Your stillness.*

297

*"In matters of conscience, the law of the majority
has no place."*
Mohandas Gandhi

How I used to hate myself. So many times
I caught myself pleasing the crowd, agreeing
with people I did not understand or respect,
laughing at jokes and opinions I loathed. How
I used to hate myself!

Today I have a healthy respect for what the
majority may feel but I also trust and follow
my conscience. I know that to be in the
minority is not necessarily to be in the wrong.
My recovery insists that I listen to my conscience, that inner self that is based on a
program of honesty, that spiritual cornerstone
of my life that I have come to trust.

Now I can say to people, "I do not agree."
Today I give myself permission to disagree with
family, friends and colleagues.

*May I never follow the crowd because of the
numbers: God is one.*

*"This land of ours cannot be a good place for any
of us to live in unless we make it a good place for
all of us to live in."*

                                        Richard Nixon

My sobriety has given me a comprehensive
view of life and my neighbor. Today I believe
that we are all connected and if I hurt or am
hurt, then everybody at some level is affected.
Because we are all children of God, it follows
that we are all one big family — speaking
different languages, having different customs,
revealing different physical characteristics and
complexions, requiring different satisfaction
(both sexual and emotional), but we are still
one big family under God.

This means I have a responsibility to all in
the family and I can best exercise that responsibility by having a healthy respect for myself.
I should treat people as I would want to be
treated, allowing them the freedom and love
I require in my life. I am the key to the world's
needs.

Lord, let me find my neighbor in myself.

*"A cynic is a man who knows the price of every-
thing and the value of nothing."*
Oscar Wilde

I never knew the value of my life until I
looked beyond it. For years I was so self-
obsessed that I missed the joy and beauty of
this wonderful world. I was so concerned with
details and the minutia of life that I missed
the fun of living.

I now see that my behavior had its roots
in my childhood. I was the child in a dysfunc-
tional family. I became a parent to my parents.
I took charge of everybody's life and I felt
responsible and guilty. Everything was work
and I did not learn how to play.

Today I am working on my recovery. I am
"dumping" my feelings of guilt, shame and
anger. I am beginning to understand that I am
not responsible for my parents and I am
beginning to feel free. Today I am learning how
to play.

Lord of the dance, teach me the steps.

"A cynic is a man who, when he smells flowers,
looks around for a coffin."
H. L. Mencken

There was a time when I always felt that life was out to get me. I always looked on the "black" side of life. I was forever being negative and pessimistic. I would always be surrounded by sick and destructive human beings. Whenever people offered hope or tried to help me, I turned away and rejected them. For years I created the pain and misery in my life.

Then a close friend forced himself into my life and gave me a dose of "tough love". He made me see that I was wallowing in self-pity. He cared enough to intervene and tell me what I did not want to hear.

Today I have some years of recovery from alcoholism and I carry the message.

I pray that I may always love myself and others
enough to take a risk.

"Better bend than break."
                                    Scottish Proverb

Dis-ease: to be controlling, stiff, uncomfortable and unbending.

Sobriety: being relaxed, comfortable and flexible in my personal life and my interaction with others.

Life: not a race but an experience; it is not an exercise but an adventure.

Before I accepted my alcoholism, I went through periods of "dryness" — when I was rigid, stiff and unbending. It was awful! Everything became a test, a job, a premeditated act behind a mask of cheerfulness. I was angry, resentful and in pain. My problem was that I stopped drinking to please other people, rather than accept the true nature of my disease. Dryness is controlled denial.

Today the sobriety I have gained from an acceptance of self has overflowed into an acceptance of life on life's terms — and I am happy.

Let the wind of experience continue to bend me in the knowledge of Your love.

"Kindness in words creates confidence. Kindness in thinking creates profoundness. Kindness in giving creates love."

Lao-tzu

It costs me nothing to say "hello" and yet it might make all the difference to my neighbor. It costs me nothing to give a hug and yet that hug might make all the difference to a friend. It costs me nothing to listen to another's pain and yet the listening might make all the difference to another person.

Love is to be found in the small, ordinary acts of kindness as well as in the extravagant gesture. I need to seek God in the everyday happenings of life alongside the "religious". Spirituality is in the smile that is real!

Today I know that I give only what I received — and I received a great deal. People loved me enough to be patient, they cared enough to telephone, they encouraged me with the gentle word of hope: I am in the flow.

Lord, You have created this wondrous patterned fabric of life — may I find You in its smallest detail.

"Justice is truth in action."
Benjamin Disraeli

It is not enough for me to believe that a thing is true, it is important for me to live out my beliefs. For too long I had a thousand beliefs that only kept me silent. A fear of displeasing others played a large part in my "lie of silence".

Today I understand justice to be part of what I mean by spirituality: I need to be seen to walk as I talk! I am uncomfortable when I remain silent in the face of injustice. As a recovering alcoholic, this "uncomfortability" is dangerous because it can so easily lead to low self-esteem, anger, resentments and relapse.

Today I know I can have a "slip" without taking a drink. I slip from where I want to be in my life. My personal integrity combines a justice that can be seen in my lifestyle.

O God of justice, teach me never again to hide in the lie of silence.

*"The finest eloquence is that which gets
things done."*
David Lloyd George

I know how to talk. I know how to sound good. I know how to convince a person of my good intentions — indeed that was part of my manipulation for years.

Today I try to walk the talk. I try to demonstrate what I say in the behavior I exhibit. The bottom line is action. Talking never stopped me from drinking — my physical refusal of the first drink was the start of my recovery.

God is to be discovered not merely in pious sentiments, as attractive as they may sound, but rather in the small steps of altered behavior.

*Am I doing what I am saying? Lord give me the
courage to live my words.*

"I want to be the white man's brother not his brother-in-law."
                              Martin Luther King, Jr.

Addiction is always about separation, ego, isolation and prejudice. The disease makes us feel different, "less than" and we cover those feelings with false humility or we assume an arrogant and bombastic manner. Pride and feelings of inferiority put us on the defensive. It is not unusual for us to seek a scapegoat for our anger. Drinking aloholics can be vindictive and prejudicial in their attitude towards minorities. Blacks, gays and Jews. It is a strange quirk of circumstance when a minority seeks to victimize another minority — because alcoholics are a minority group!

Sobriety is about a change in attitude and behavior. The spiritual acceptance of self must lead inevitably to the acceptance of others. The false pride and arrogance of our drinking days must give way to the vulnerable strength of sobriety. Now we are able to embrace our brother, regardless of color, class or creed.

Lord, teach me to seek You in my fellow man and greet You in the stranger.

"Seeing is deceiving. It's eating that's believing."
                                    James Thurber

It may seem strange to many but for years my belief system revolved around my eating. I believed that if I could eat I would be okay. Food for me was both the pleasure and escape. I lived to eat. Feelings, good and bad, were surrounded and stuffed down with food. Some people drank to hide, used cocaine to escape — I ate to avoid the problems in my life.

Seeing was deceiving for me because I refused to accept the reality of my eating. I covered myself with clothes, avoided the beach, rarely looked at my body. I saw only what I wanted to see — and I was dying. Now I choose to face reality. This for me is the meaning of spirituality. I choose to show my love for me by loving my food, making choices around what I eat and eating slowly. Today I choose to talk about my problems, rather than eat them.

God, help me to accept my daily bread with gratitude and abstinence.

> *"Every saint has a past and every sinner*
> *a future."*
>
> *Oscar Wilde*

I must not allow the painful things of my past to affect what I can do today. Guilt is a killer if I allow it power in my life. I have made my amends. I have apologized to those I hurt. Today I begin the rest of my life.

Alcoholism produces behavior that causes guilt and shame. In this sense it is different from so many other diseases. The shame and guilt I felt for years grew out of my alcoholic behavior and I need to remember that I am not responsible for being alcoholic. It is not my fault. However, with the knowledge and acceptance of the disease comes a determination to live responsibly. I have a sense of responsibility in my recovery. Spirituality involves being a responsible person. The awareness and acceptance of my past can help create a loving future.

Today I understand that in the failures of the past
are sown the seeds of greatness.

Gluttony is not a secret vice.

Orson Welles

*"Appeasers believe that if you keep on throwing
steaks to tigers, the tiger will become
a vegetarian."*
                              Heywood Broun

Spirituality involves taking risks. But the risk
has to be sensible, having the possibility of
success. The risks I take today have a chance,
usually a good chance, of succeeding and I
always discuss "the risk" with a sponsor or
recovering friend with some years of sobriety.

Today I take risks on things and situations
that have the possibility of working *for* me,
rather than *against* me. God has given me
freedom and He has taken a risk on how I
exercise that freedom. God's love is revealed
in the risk. But risk should have the possibility
of success!

I pray that I will continue to take sensible risks.

"In solitude, be a multiple of thyself."
Tibullus

When I am alone and still, I get in touch with that side of me that is "the many". There are so many sides to me; the crazy and the sane, the extrovert and the introvert; the demanding and the submissive; the bigot and the compassionate; the religious and the sceptic; the happy and the sad; the comic and the tragedian; the child and the adult; the sick and the recovering.

Today in the silence of solitude I experience the many sides of me that I must live with — this is my spiritual reality.

May I always use my multiple experiences to relate and understand others.

"Another good reducing exercise consists in placing both hands against the table edge and pushing back."

                                        Robert Quillen

I am an alcoholic and today I choose not to drink. When alcohol is offered, I say "no". I do not go into "wet places", spend time with drinkers or put myself in awkward situations. I assist my abstinence by the choices I make.

The recovering gambler avoids Las Vegas. The drug addict avoids sick relationships. The compulsive overeater must exercise the spiritual power of choice around food. "No" must involve both hands! For the recovering addict, talk must be accompanied by action. Some people, places and things must be avoided.

Spirituality is making my talk a visible reality.

"I hear and I forget. I see and I remember. I do and I understand."

Chinese Proverb

I suppose the best way to learn a thing is to do it, practice it, demonstrate it, make it real in our live. Spirituality needs to be experienced, not talked about. You cannot learn spirituality, get spirituality from a famous guru, read and acquire spirituality from a book — spirituality needs to be discovered in our lives. It needs to be found in body, sexuality, sweat, anger, morning exercise and kneeling in prayer and gratitude at the end of the day.

God, may You be real in my life.

*"The spirit of liberty . . . is the spirit which is
not too sure it is always right."*
Judge Learned Hand

I am free to make mistakes. It is okay for
me to be wrong. I can say or do something
that proves to be incorrect. I am not perfect.

Part of the liberty of being a human being
is not being perfect; I am not God. In a sense
this is a relief. I do not have to take responsibility for the lives of others or the crises in
the world. It is okay not to have all the answers.
Indeed, sometimes the spiritual life is discovered in "not knowing" and the answer will
forever remain in the question. It is human
to ask "why are we like we are?" But the answer
rests in God.

*God of Reason, let me be satisfied with discovering
You in the questions.*

*"An atheist is a man who has no invisible means
of support."*

John Buchanan

The common cry of those who suffer from
addiction is that they feel isolated. Not only
isolated from self, family and friends but also
from God. One reason for this feeling of
isolation is teachings and attitudes that produced guilt, shame and fear. God was seen as
a hammer with which society beat the addict.

Today, in an atmosphere of love and fellowship, we begin to look at these old attitudes
and, hopefully, begin to change them. God can
be seen in the hug as well as the sacrament;
in the doubt as well as the dogma. In the honest
sharing of fellow addicts, God is made known.
God needs to be given a human face.

*Teach me to grow in the virtues of tolerance and
understanding.*

*"A good scare is worth more to a man than
good advice."*

Ed Howe

My fear of alcoholism helped me into treatment. My awareness of reality — "I am an
alcoholic," — helped me towards recovery. I
was scared into treatment!

I must never forget my frightening yesterdays
because that can so easily lead to minimization
and tomorrow's denial. I need to remember my
pain if I am to continue to gain. My car
accident, my abuse of self and others, my
suicidal behavior should be feared, on a daily
basis, because it is only one drink away!

God has given me a memory — I need to
use it. My spiritual courage is in remembering
my yesterdays so that I can continue to enjoy
the sobriety of today.

*May I see that a healthy fear comes from God; it
is part of His love for me.*

*"There is no place in active life on which thought
is negligible."*

T. S. Eliot

It is not a crime to think. It is not a sin
to have a brain. To think is human.

However, so much of my past thinking was
destructive and negative. The disease of
addiction permeated every aspect of my life —
particularly my thoughts. For years my best
ideas justified my addiction.

Today I am open to a change of mind. I can
choose to change my ideas. I am free to think
differently.

God is alive in my willingness to change.

Lord, help my thinking to recover.

"Adversity is the trial of principle. Without it a man hardly knows whether he is honest or not."
                                        Henry Fielding

The acceptance of my disease has brought me into recovery. If I had not known and confronted the disease of addiction in my life, I would not know the joys of sobriety and serenity. Spirituality involves facing my disease.

Today I believe that had I not seen my dishonesty, I could not fully appreciate honesty. If I had not recognized the lies and games in my life, I could never have appreciated the "openness" and freedom of sobriety. Owning my violence brought me to peace and tolerance. Facing my hell gave me a glimpse of paradise.

The disease was not only my prison but when accepted, became the key to recovery. Spirituality, finding God in our lives, requires a "rigorous honesty" that uses the past pain to experience today's gratitude.

God, it is through the acceptance of my failings that I can love the world.

"Faith is never identical with piety."
                                        Karl Barth

Drugs make us artificial and unreal. They create a world of fantasy, rather than reality and teach us how to escape rather than live. Everything is exaggerated and dehumanized — especially the practice of our religion. Often for the addict, religion becomes part of the escape, a ritual that becomes exaggerated and theatrical, expecting magic rather than miracle.

Madonnas are kissed, promises are made, confessions become routine, prayers are mouthed and God is manipulated with the disease. Piety, the religious art of showmanship, keeps us a prisoner of the small "god".

Faith takes seriously our pain and isolation and promises recovery only with change and accepted responsibility. We must walk our prayers and live our rosary!

O God, build Your temple in my heart and Your altar in my daily sacrifice of love to self and others.

"Peace without justice is tyranny."
                    William Allen White

Peace at any price! Not for me today. For years I sought a peace that was based upon the "no-talk" principle — remaining quiet, rather than causing upset or risking embarrassment. Such a peace was unjust. It only fed the disease and helped to keep me sick.

Today I seek a peace that involves discussing or confronting painful situations, often making me and others uncomfortable. Serenity is a peace that is arrived at after periods of pain — but a necessary pain.

In my life today I have the courage to speak out and make choices that are good for me; God is alive in my choice.

May I forever search for the "peace" that is real.
May I find "peace" in the justice
of my lifestyle.

"It is the test of a good religion if you can joke about it."

G. K. Chesterton

Today I am able to joke with God and about God. I am able to laugh at me swinging incense at a candlestick — and then swinging the incense at the Bishop! I smile at the determined seriousness of choirboys who receive communion while at the same time sticking chewing gum under the arm rail. I chuckle at the embarrassment of the baptism family when the baby pulls the plug out of the font and the holy water drains away.

Today I am able to laugh at God and His Church — it joyously reflects man's imperfection but at the same time reminds him of his glory.

God, I contemplate You laughing at our pompous piety.

"Money doesn't always bring happiness. People with ten million dollars are no happier than people with nine million dollars."

Hobart Brown

Today I understand that there is nothing intrinsically wrong with money. Wealth is not good or bad in itself — it is what we do with it. As a famous comedian once said, "I've been rich and I've been poor — and rich is better!"

But in what sense is rich better? I suppose in the freedom that it affords us, not only to travel and buy comfortable "things" but also in the way we can help and contribute to the lives and well-being of others. But to hoard money, be "stingy" with yourself and others, make a "god" of possessions or become compulsive about the "making of money" produces the same pain as any other addiction.

Money is to be used. It is usually one of the benefits of sobriety, part of what it means to say "it gets better". Why? Because we are more responsible and creative as sober people and this brings its rewards.

Help me to be a responsible steward of the possessions You entrusted to me.

*"It is seldom that an American retires from
business to enjoy his fortune in comfort . . .
He works because he has always worked,
and knows no other way."*

                                        Thomas Nichols

For years I rushed around being busy — and
I missed me. I spent years trying to please
people by doing things — and I missed me. I
was a workaholic, my value was seen only in
what I could achieve — and I missed me.

Today I can relax in my sobriety; indeed
sobriety has enabled me to relax. I can sit and
do nothing and it is okay. Life is about "being"
and not "doing". Spirituality is about taking
time out for me because I am worth it. "Be
still and know that I am God," said the
psalmist. In the silence of self I have discovered
the meaning of life and I have found God.

*Thank You, Lord, for creating the feelings of peace
that come from leisure.*

*"No man knows of what stuff he is made until
prosperity and ease try him."*

A.P. Gouthey

I must be careful that I do not get too comfortable and self-confident. I must be careful that I do not plateau at this stage of my journey into sobriety and relax in past achievements. Sometimes I hear the disease of addiction saying to me, "You've done all you need — now relax; take it easy."

Sometimes the sick voice says, "Listen to the stupidity of these newly recovering people: avoid them! " "You don't need meetings now — just sit and talk with your friends." Historically I know that when things are going well for me, that is when I need to be careful. A complacent and indulgent sobriety is dangerous. It leads to the disarming slip of arrogance and false pride.

I need to remember the pain of my yesterdays; I need to hear the newly recovering; I need to hear the pain if I am to continue to gain. My disease will forever speak, but will I listen?

*Teach me to embrace a humility that enables me to
enjoy a realistic sobriety.*

*"True friendship comes when silence between two
people is comfortable."*
                    Dave Tyson Gentry

Part of the spiritual life that awakens
serenity is silence or stillness. "Be still and know
that I am God." I believe that true friendship
is divine. It is a special love that binds two
hearts as one. It is a comfortableness that is
the opposite of dis-ease. Friendship is necessary
to recovery and it involves the sharing of
feelings. Often the feelings are silent; unspoken
emotions; cherished moments that exist in
"word-less-ness".

As a recovering alcoholic, I have a thousand
friends who attest to the silent witness of love
by simply being there.

*Thank You for the joy of friendship that grows
in silence.*

*"Experience is not what happens to a man. It is
what a man does with what happens to him."*
                                        Aldous Huxley

Today I experience the joy of sobriety. Today
I experience God in my world. Today I experience the peace and serenity that for years
eluded me.

Experience is the key. It locates all that is
in my life. Experience allows me to appreciate
what living is all about.

Love is to be felt. Forgiveness is to be
experienced. Humility is to be lived in action.
Hope is to be recognized in the brightness of
the eye.

Life is to be experienced. That is spirituality.

*May the God that I experience be reflected in my
daily life.*

"All cruelty springs from weakness."
                                        Seneca

My spiritual recovery means that I confront my disease and remember sick attitudes and behavior patterns. I would rather not talk about my disease because it is embarrassing and shameful — particularly my cruelty to people and animals. My alcoholism made me lash out at the weak; yes, my weakness inflicted pain and cruelty on others.

I remember this only to rejoice in today's strength that allows vulnerability. My past weaknesses made me act strong. Today my strength allows me to be weak.

God, the recognition of my past cruelties enables me to forgive and understand others.

"He that cannot forgive others breaks the bridge over which he must pass himself. For every man has need to be forgiven."

                                  Thomas Fuller

My failings as an alcoholic help me to live with others today. The fact that I made and make mistakes helps me to have creative relationships today. Because I know what it is to fail, I can understand the failings of others. My weaknesses are a bridge to understanding my fellow man.

By contrast when I was drinking, I thought I was perfect, always right and this led to judgments, arguments and a self-imposed alienation.

Alcohol fed my arrogance and pride; sobriety helps develop humility and understanding.

God, I understand that even my failings can be made to work for me in sobriety.

"When I want to understand what is happening today or try to decide what will happen tomorrow, I look back."
                    Oliver Wendell Holmes, Jr.

The writing is on the wall! My writing is on my wall and it is to be found in my life. My history of my life teaches me about my alcoholism. Alcoholism is a personal disease; it affects others through self.

Sometimes I am tempted to forget the past. Why live in yesterday? Because the events of my yesterdays affect my today. The future is forged from the recognition of my past. My disease grew strong in my denial. My recovery began with the acceptance of reality — my reality.

Today does not exist in a vacuum and my tomorrows are determined by the decisions I make today. I also know and believe that my recovering life demands a true recognition of my yesterdays.

Thank You for the historical progressiveness of my recovery.

"Self-trust is the essence of heroism."
Ralph Waldo Emerson

In my recovery I have become my hero. It sounds egotistical but it is part of my program of self-love. I have many other heroes but today I respect myself. Today I believe that God is involved in my life; an aspect of divinity exists within me. I trust me with my life, and I am proud of the daily choices I make for my sobriety.

Spirituality allows me to be my hero today because it is with my respect of self that I can truly respect others; the awareness of my dignity affords dignity to others; my personal healing brings healing to others.

Today I am the center of my universe.

Thank You for the awareness of the achievements and successes in my life; today I am my own winner.

"Obesity is really widespread."
                              Joseph O. Kern II

To be fat is to be lost. It is a self-imposed isolation that keeps people sad. The fat is the result of an addiction to a series of chemicals in food that society finds acceptable; the disease of bulimia is widespread.

But it can be changed. People can and do get well from a compulsion around food by surrendering to the reality of their compulsion. The people-pleasing must be seen. The mask must be removed. The pain in the family must be talked about. Feelings that have been buried behind the food for years should be expressed. Feelings are to be felt!

We need not remain fat, and recovery begins when we begin to have hope; we begin to love ourselves; we begin to believe in ourselves.

O Lord, You hear the prayer of all Your children
    — help me to hear my prayers, too!

"History is the seed bed of the future."
Leo Booth

I talk about my drinking history, remembering the incidents and losses, because I believe "there is no gain without pain". To enjoy my sobriety I must share, on a daily basis, the reality of my disease. My pain is rooted in my history. I must live with my disease on a daily basis. I need to be aware of the disease process in my life.

This awareness requires a "rigorously honest" inventory of my past attitudes and behaviors; ignorance is bliss for the disease of addiction! The acceptance and awareness of my past is my treatment for today. The more I understand about my yesterdays the better my recovery will be today. My life has a history and my spiritual program demands that I understand it.

Teach me to face my past so that I can realistically live in my today.

*"If we are not ashamed to think it, we should not
be ashamed to say it."*
Marcus Tullius Cicero

I was afraid to tell you what I was thinking.
I was afraid to speak or be noticed. I sat for
hours silent and at times I wished I could vanish
into the furniture. I was afraid of my shadow.

This reveals not only my lack of confidence
but my low self-esteem. I did not think I had
anything to say, anything to offer, anything
that might be considered interesting. I would
laugh at stupid things to please people.

Today I speak out. I do not hide what I am
thinking. I believe I have something to offer
in the celebration of life. And it feels good.
My spiritual growth is proportionate to my
willingness to let you know who I am and what
I think.

I celebrate my joy in living by sharing it.

*"I am an idealist. I don't know where I am going
but I'm on my way."*
Carl Sandburg

Today I am on the move. I feel an energy
in my life that gets excited each day. New
people, new places, new ideas all give me "a
spiritual charge" that help me enjoy my life.

I don't have all the answers and sometimes
I am confused — but today I can live with
this and enjoy it. God seems to reveal Himself
more in the questions rather than the answers;
it is the problems that produce the growth.

The journey of my life is an adventure that
is free and unchartered, even the pain and
problems produce a benefit that can be used
for my recovery. Nothing need be wasted.

I am the Way.
I am the Truth.
I am the Light.

*"There is a destiny that makes us brothers, none
goes his way alone. All that we send into the lives
of others comes back into our own."*
                                        Edwin Markham

I can remember when I felt so isolated and
alone. I used to look at people talking with
their friends, families playing in the park, lovers
holding hands, and I felt so different and
awkward. I always looked at life from the
outside. I was the guy without an invitation
to the party. The symptoms of addiction!

Today I know that my actions and behavior
around alcohol reinforced these negative and
destructive feelings. By my drinking I was
perpetuating the painful disease in my life.

Sobriety led me into fellowship with others;
it brought me into the family of recovering
people. Today I am not alone. I have over a
million brothers and sisters living a day at a
time in a spiritual program. I have countless
thousands finding joy, peace and serenity in
sister programs. Today I belong in this world.

*O God, thank You for giving me the need to give
so that I might receive.*

"Whenever science makes a discovery, the devil grabs it while the angels are debating the best way to use it."

Alan Valentine

Sometimes we can spend so long deciding what to do that we miss an opportunity. We can prevaricate to the point of impotence. Nowhere is this more true than in the science of relationships. We see somebody that we like and we go home thinking about what we could have said or done. We create happenings in our mind that never happened in fact. We miss the spiritual opportunity of risk.

For years I used to be like this. I always thought that I was not good enough, not important, less than other people: the syndrome of low self-esteem.

Today it is getting better. Part of my spiritual growth is reaching out to other people. Today I make a point of saying "hello". Today I will ask for a telephone number, invite people to dinner, risk a relationship.

Let me not debate myself into sickness and isolation.

"The certainties of one age are the problems of the next."

R. H. Tawney

I was a religious bigot. I did not know that I was a bigot, but now I see how closed and narrow my thinking was. I craved for certainty because I felt it would give me security and happiness — but it never did. I argued dogmas that I did not believe: the plight of the unhappy hypocrite!

Today I live only in the certainty of the day. Today I know that what worked for me yesterday will work for me today if I am open to love, truth, honesty and change. Change is not necessarily "difference" if I see it as part of a process rather than an event. Yesterday is linked to today, and together they forge tomorrow. The one thing of which I can be certain is change. The God of Truth is revealed in the change; the acceptance of this fact is spirituality.

May I continue to grow in the spiritual life by my continued desire to change and be tolerant.

"Men become civilized, not in proportion to their willingness to believe, but in their readiness to doubt."

H. L. Mencken

A civilized nation is essentially a spiritual nation. A civilized person is one who seeks the truth and is willing to grow with change.

Sobriety is adventuresome because it is bigger than simply "not drinking"; it seeks to address all areas of life and all situations. An example is trust. When I was drinking, I trusted no one because I felt that everybody was like me — out for themselves! Today I know that the real enemy in my life is me; I am the one who brings pain into my life. I am beginning to love myself by my decision not to drink. I can trust today. I am beginning to trust myself and others.

O God, who trusted man with freedom, help me to freely trust.

"I am the master of my fate;
I am the captain of my soul."
                                        William E. Henley

Things do not just happen, we make them
happen. For years I thought that my getting
well was dependent upon my family getting
well. I rooted my recovery in the recovery of
others. I was the typical co-dependent.

Then somebody said, "Why don't you start
taking responsibility for your own life?" I
thought about that remark for weeks. I spent
nights dwelling on the implications of those
words. I am sure that I had heard similar
sentiments a hundred times but that night,
that special night, I was ready to hear them.
A spiritual moment.

Today I believe that such spiritual moments
produce a spiritual process that I must keep
alive. I am the deciding factor in what happens
to me and what I can achieve. God has created
me to be involved in my recovery.

May I always steer my life in the direction of
truth and love.

*"Great minds discuss ideas, average minds discuss
wants, small minds discuss people."*
                                    Laurence J. Peter

Gossip is ultimately a form of malicious
cowardice. It is a "blasphemy" because it seeks
to denigrate the human being that God has
made in His image.

As a practicing alcoholic I was a gossip. I
exaggerated and manipulated the truth with
my gossip. I made up stories against those
people I had a resentment towards; innocent
people were abused and victimized by my
gossip.

Also I loved listening to gossip. The listener
plays an important role in the life of "gossip"
because without the listener it could not exist.
It takes two to gossip!

Today gossip is unacceptable behavior in my
program.

*Teach me Master to reach beyond my "smallness"
into Your greatness.*

"The certainties of one age are the problems of the next."

         R. H. Tawney

Life is a process of change that inevitably produces problems; the fear of the new, the discomfort of old values being seen to be wrong, the confusion that so often accompanies growth. Problems are part of life and we can only escape them in death. (Even then nobody can be sure we will be free of problems!)

As an alcoholic I tried to run away from my problems by drinking. But the next day the old problems were still there and my drinking had usually brought new problems. Alcohol only produced a momentary escape but reality always returned.

Today, with the acceptance of my alcoholism and my decision not to "pick up the first drink", I face my problems. I deal with my problems. I live with the problems of life.

Teach me to accept joyously the problems that life and growth inevitably bring.

*"Wonder rather than doubt is the root of
knowledge."*
                              Abraham Heschel

Living with paradox is part of my sobriety.
Things are never quite what they seem. When
I think I have something figured out, I am made
to be confused again — especially around my
life, relationships, people, events and the
universe. Life is both simple and incomprehensible. God seems to demand an agnostic faith!
There is so much I do not know or understand.

But all of this leads to a creative and exciting
sobriety. It makes life an adventure. It feeds
that artistic part of me that is reborn in my
sobriety. Things I used to dislike when I drank,
I now enjoy. People and writers that once bored
me now fascinate me; even modern art has a
spiritual message!

*O God, let the feelings of amazement always be a
part of my faith.*

"Everyone is a prisoner of his own experiences. No one can eliminate prejudices —
just recognize them."
                                    Edward R. Murrow

In recovery I am accepting that I am not perfect and some prejudices are part of my life — what it is to be human. On a daily basis I am trying to deal with them, and talking about them helps. They don't go away just because I talk about them, but I get them in perspective and I grow in an understanding of myself through the recognition of my prejudices.

Alcoholism made me into a "fake". I appeared to be what I was not and my prejudices were part of the camouflage. My prejudices revealed my fears and my need to "people-please". Slowly, in my daily spiritual program, I am discovering the courage to stand alone.

Teach me to love truth more than popularity.

*"Not every woman in old slippers can manage to
look like Cinderella."*

Don Marquis

Beauty is not what you wear or look like;
beauty is within. We begin to love ourselves
when we see the beauty that God has given
to each and every one of us — forever. God's
image and beauty is expressed through our
attitudes and feelings, how we greet and listen
to each other and the gentle dignity we afford
to another human being.

For years I saw myself as ugly, boring, useless
and stupid. This message came from parents
who forever compared me with others — and
for years I believed their message. I hid through
my teen-age years and quietly tried to escape
in food, alcohol and drugs.

Then after a crisis I met people who had
felt the same but were now feeling different.
They loved me until I could begin to love
myself. Now I like me. Now I can love me.
Today I can like and love you.

*Help me to see the beauty in the wrinkle; the
power in the pain.*

"There are two kinds of failures: those who thought and never did, and those who did and never thought."
                                    Laurence J. Peter

In my life I know that I am guilty of both these failures. I remember making sandcastles in the air without realizing that I could attempt to build one in my life. I would see somebody I wanted to talk with and imagine a conversation, rather than going over and risking possible rejection. Today I am able to risk — and I am now the possessor of a thousand memories that actually happened.

I am also aware of how thoughtless I was in my addiction. I would react rather than respond; create hostility as a wall to keep people out. Today I am able to think through a problem and apologize when I am wrong.

O Lord, You have made us to live in a world of happenings. Help us to accept the richness of life on its terms.

*"Man is a complex being: he makes deserts bloom
 — and lakes die."*

Gil Stern

I am a mixture of good and bad. When I
was drinking I could be cruel, sarcastic and
violent and at other times loving, sensitive and
thoughtful. Today in my recovery I know I can
be honest, humble and creative, but I also carry
within me a dark and destructive side that
often hurts, lies and seeks negative power.
What a mixture I was and what a mixture I
still am! From all my many conversations with
a variety of people I have discovered that this
is what it is to be human.

Today I am able to accept this and develop
my spiritual life. I am not perfect, but I try
to improve my attitude and behavior. I am not
God, but I can aspire to be the best that I
can be.

Today I own the sickness in my life, but I
also accept the responsibility for recovery.

With my feet in the dirt, I look to the stars.

*"All animals, except man, know that the ultimate
of life is to enjoy it."*

                        Samuel Butler

Today I choose to enjoy my life. Regardless
of the problems and difficulties that this day
will bring, I have an inner joy that comes with
my recovery from addiction. With a clear head
and body — free from drugs and chemicals —
I can face today and look forward to tomorrow.
My life is to be enjoyed not endured. My worst
days today are better than my best days as an
addict. Spiritually I am free because I have
begun to discover me. God can now be perceived in His world because I have sobriety.

*Lord of all play, I dance before You in my world
and I can stop to smell the roses.*

*"Growing old isn't so bad when you consider the
alternative."*
                                    Maurice Chevalier

What is the alternative? Not to change! To
stay rooted in adolescence, youth, middle-age
or whatever. Not to age is not to live, not to
experience and not to grow spiritually.

An aspect of age, for which I am beginning
to be grateful, is "comparison"; today I am able
to look at the past and see the benefits of the
present. Growth is measurable only through
the tunnel of age. I suppose my fear of age
is my basic fear of the "unkown"; fear of
"unmanageability" and "powerlessness".

These words remind me of the spiritual
program that teaches me to confidently place
my life in the loving arms of God. If I am
responsible in life, I will be responsible in old
age.

*Teach me to use the spiritual perspective that
comes with the gift of age.*

*"There is no higher religion than human service.
To work for the common good is
the greatest creed."*

Albert Schweitzer

I enjoy doing things for other people. I enjoy seeing other people happy, seeing gratitude in their eyes and experiencing their hug of thankfulness.

Some people need to restrict how much they do for others and begin doing more for themselves — but I am happy and pleased with my service towards others. Why? Because I used to be a "taker". For years I would walk away with all that you could give me and only thank you because I wanted to return for more!

In sobriety I am beginning to change this. Now I am giving and I am enjoying it.

Lord, the gift of service is a precious gift.

"The only courage that matters is the kind that gets you from one moment to the next."
                    Mignon McLaughlin

I do not have to have courage for a life time, just for the moment. I am helped by the philosophy that teaches me to live one day at a time, one hour at a time, one moment at a time. It is too awesome to try to live my tomorrows today. Life is a process to be lived not a future to be anticipated.

For years I tried to anticipate what life had to throw at me, and I always came away confused, surprised and exhausted. I missed the joy of the moment by worrying about the future. What was he going to do? What happens if the police get involved? Will my mother telephone next week? Will my niece grow up to be alcoholic? Am I to blame? I had a thousand questions that I could not answer; nobody can answer for the future today.

I can only take responsibility for my life a day at a time. I developed the courage to face the moment and I became a winner.

May I avoid the temptation to seek the fantasy of tomorrow for the reality of today.

"At the back of every noble life are the principles
that have fashioned it."
George Lorimer

God is to be found in the principles of life.
The suggested patterns of behavior that lead
to happiness, freedom and unity in the world.
God is not just a "good idea", an intellectual
philosophy or other worldly entity — God is
practical goodness that can be demonstrated
and seen in the world. Principles lead to action;
principles produce change in attitude and
behavior; principles must have a practical
result.

Sometimes you hear the phrase "walk the
talk", implying that the principles we talk
about should be evident in our daily lives. Also
principles should be seen in the small things
of life — being courteous, giving a smile to
a stranger, offering a hug to a friend in pain.
God is alive in the principles of life.

Help me to practice the principles I believe in.

"Man cannot remake himself without suffering.
For he is both the marble and the sculptor."
                                        Alexis Carrel

I know that I have grown through my
sufferings. I know that I am able to understand
and forgive other people because I have been
there, too. I know that I am patient and
considerate because of my sufferings. My
anguish keeps me "earthed". It stops me from
playing God; it teaches me the reality of life
— that life hurts! It is wonderful, joyous, loving
and eventful, but it also hurts. For many years
I hid my sufferings and pretended they were
not there; the result was loneliness and hypocrisy.

Today I accept my sufferings and share them.
I am finding out that I need not be lonely or
hide behind the mask of hypocrisy.

God, may my sufferings keep me real.

"My God, my God, why hast thou forsaken me."
                              Jesus (Matthew 27:46)

In my sickness I was often angry at God.
Angry that He did not do what I wanted Him
to do when I wanted Him to do it. I was a
spoiled child. I refused to understand that
suffering could be an important part of my
spiritual growth. Today I know this to be true.

The biggest part of my suffering, then and
today, is the feeling of isolation. Not knowing
for certain that He hears me. Not understanding completely what His will is for me. Not
getting clear answers to my daily confusion.

The doubt is part of the faith. The "not
knowing" is the answer.

Lord, may the daily doubts lead to a creative faith.

"The poor you always have with you."
                              Jesus (John 12:8)

Whoever said that life was going to be easy?
A great number of people are placed in circumstances that are beyond their control and
they die in helpless poverty. The poor are
always with us. I cannot understand this
dilemma and I have few answers for most of
the world's suffering. However, I have a faith
in God's love being realized beyond the grave
for everyone.

But many of "the poor" are spiritually
destitute by their own making. They choose
to live lives that are consistently destructive
and they refuse to change. Alcoholics and drug
addicts are committing suicide by their lifestyle!
I know because for years I was one. This
produces a spiritual poverty that need not
remain. This is a poverty that can be overcome.
Recovery is finding the hidden treasure that
is within.

Let me find Your treasure in the loving care
I give myself.

"Liberty is the one thing you can't have unless you give it to others."

William Allen White

Spirituality is rooted in a respect for self that demands an equal respect for others. I can expect to be treated with dignity if I afford dignity to others. In the one is the key to the many.

For years I lived a compulsive life that only made me self-centered and spoiled, and it didn't work! I was unhappy, lonely and resentful. Today I find that the more I give to others the more I receive. Less is more.

In this sense it is much easier to be good than bad because "goodness" works!

Spirit of generosity, may I always reflect the gratitude that gives.

*"Nothing in life is to be feared. It is only
to be understood."*

                           Marie Curie

God is on my side. Today I really believe
and understand this truth, and it helps me cope
with my fears. Now I am beginning to understand that I was the only real enemy in my
life. With this new understanding of God I
have the power of choice back in my life.

I do not have to stay in a sick process. I
do not need sick and negative people in my
life. I do not have to place myself in destructive
relationships or in fearful situations. God is
alive in my life and I am discovering the
spiritual power of choice.

*God, give me the courage to confront my fear and
be willing to make changes in my life.*

"You are free and that is why you are lost."
                                    Franz Kafka

Part of my understanding of spirituality is that we have many choices and we live in moments of "not knowing". Part of being human is that we have feelings of being lost. These feelings can lead to fear and loneliness or they can be seen as the essence of man's risk and adventure. With freedom comes daily uncertainties; nothing is predestined or made to happen — God is in the choice. Herein lies true greatness. The fact is that we do not have all the answers. We are not sure of the results. The joys are mingled with the pain and sorrows — such is the divinity of life. And yet still we choose to live!

Sobriety is accepting the reality of this uncertain life. My responsibility is accepting this freedom and making a daily choice not to drink.

May I accept my "lostness" until I return home to You.

*"The People, though we think a great entity when
we use the word, means nothing more than so
many millions of individual men (and women)."*
                                        James Bryce

I am an individual. I am unique. I am special.
Today I am able to enjoy my difference. I do
not need to hide in alcohol, food or drugs. I
do not have to put energy into being the same
as friends or neighbors. I do not need to please
people in order to feel good about myself.
Today I am my own person.

God made us varied and different in so many
ways, and yet so many of us spend our time
trying to be the same. The effort exerted to
achieve the lowest common denominator is
exactly that: the lowest. My spiritual program
demands that I be honest with who I am and
what I feel. My self-worth is rooted in my
individuality. In my difference is my soul.

May I always remain true to my individuality.

"Pessimist: One who, when he has the choice of two evils, chooses both."

Oscar Wilde

Today I am able to see how I was always looking on the "gloomy" side of life. The glass was always half empty! I can remember thinking that nothing good was ever going to happen, life was to be endured, everybody had a price and people were all selfishly out for themselves.

I projected onto others my own sickness, my own despair, my own pessimism. It was a suicidal existence. Today I choose to be a positive and creative person who refuses to be surrounded by negativism. My attitude in life makes all the difference to my enjoyment of life. Today my glass is more than half full and I am happy.

In the gift of choice, I recognize my potential joy.

"Originality exists in every individual because each of us differ from the others. We are all primary numbers divisible only by ourselves."
                                        Jean Guitton

For too many years I tried to be "the same" as other people; matched their styles, repeated their words, did what they wanted, lived to please a crowd of people I did not really know — and they certainly did not know me! I said other people's prayers, quoted other people's opinions and memorized the ideas of others — and I felt empty.

Today I value the lives of others but I am slowly beginning to explore my place in this universe. Today I accept the "specialness" that is me; that uniqueness makes me God's miracle. Now others are listening and benefiting from my life.

O God, in my difference I am discovering my service.

"Great works are performed, not by strength, but perseverance."

Samuel Johnson

Today I saw a large 200-pound man drunk in a parking lot. Last night I heard a frail mother celebrate ten years of sobriety. The difference? Perseverance. People get what they really want in life. If you want sobriety more than anything else, are prepared to go to any lengths, then nothing will stop you. Perseverance reveals the "walk" as well as the "talk".

Today I need to remember that what is worth having requires sacrifice and effort. God helps those who are prepared to help themselves. Today I intend to help myself to sobriety.

I pray that I may persevere through my fears towards my goal.

> *"If thought corrupts language, language can also corrupt thought."*
>
> *George Orwell*

Sobriety for me means much more than "not drinking" or "not using" — it means the daily decision to be a positive and creative human being in all areas of my life: How I treat people. What I eat. The books I read — and how I speak! Not even my worst enemy would call me a "prude" but I think that bad language used on a regular basis is unacceptable in sobriety. Why? Because it hurts the listener and does not show respect for self or the God-given gift of communication.

If you have no respect for language, you will ultimately not grow as a spiritual person.

May Your "words of love" be reflected in my speech and writings.

"I am a citizen, not of Athens or Greece, but of the world."

Socrates

My recovery has enabled me to see that I belong; I belong not simply to a race or nation but to the world. The freedom experienced in my recovery enables me to embrace different cultures, races and religions. Spirituality has brought harmony into my life.

Today I can go where I please. I can learn languages and communicate with people in foreign lands. I can listen to ideas and philosophies that enrich God "as I understand Him". The healing that I have experienced in my recovery is more than discovering my choice around alcohol, it is discovering my choice around life. Today I am not content to exist in my life, I choose to live it. Welcome to my world!

May I always choose to see and appreciate the richness of my life.

> *"And the Word was made flesh and dwelt*
> *amongst us."*
>
> John (1:14)

There is a beautiful fairy tale about a land where everybody had an abundance of "warm fuzzies" that they exchanged with each other and shared with each other. Everything in this land was wonderful because all the people were generously giving and receiving "warm fuzzies".

Then a rumor began that there was to be a shortage of "warm fuzzies," and people began to hoard and selfishly protect their supply of "warm fuzzies." At this point, "cold pricklies" were introduced into the land. Sadness, pain, tension and persecution developed in the land, and the growth of the "cold pricklies" kept people separated, fearful and alone.

The tragedy of this tale is that the rumor was not true! As long as people generously share their "warm fuzzies", they will never disappear. The "warm fuzzies" only disappear when they are not shared. The more we give, the more we receive. Abundance rests in giving, never hoarding!

Master, may I always be generous with all that
You have given me.

> *"The only thing necessary for the triumph of evil is for good men to do nothing."*
> Edmund Burke

I read about the Holocaust and I am ashamed. I am ashamed to belong to the human race that allowed, by an overwhelming silence, the slaughter of millions. The ultimate in people-pleasing is to do nothing. The fear of being an outcast or traitor allows the addiction to Power to develop. Power is an addiction that is rarely discussed in society. And yet evil needs people and politics to function — alone it is but a word.

With this new day I seek to be involved in the good life. Today I am not afraid to stand alone for what I believe to be the principles of a God-given spirituality. I know evil because I know myself. I know tyranny and injustice because for years I perpetrated negativity in my life. Now I choose to say "no". Today I seek to make amends for past wrongs by being rigorously honest in all my affairs. Because I know what it is to hate, I seek to love. I wish to be responsible in God's world.

Teach me not only to learn from past mistakes but translate this knowledge into action.

"Sin has many tools, but a lie is the handle that fits them all."
                                    Oliver Wendell Holmes

To lie is to rob life of meaning. In my addiction I was a liar, not just by what I said but by what I did, what I left unsaid and by my manipulation with half-truths. All lies shut out truth making us prisoners of fantasy and illusion. The world becomes what we want it to be, rather than what it is — and reality is lost. The liar is forced into the prison of loneliness, despair and isolation because nobody can know him, nobody can understand him. His language and communication are ego-centered. The liar is not living in the real world. He is living in his own world, with his own rules and definitions. The lies are the killing wounds, and they are self-inflicted.

Today I prefer the pain of truth to the passing satisfaction of the lie — and the habit of telling the truth is growing in me!

God of Truth, may You ever be reflected in the life I seek to live.

*"Humor is an affirmation of dignity, a declaration
of man's superiority to all that befalls him."*
                                                    Romain Gary

Today I laugh at myself. Today I need to
laugh at myself in order to stay sane. Today
I choose not to take myself too seriously.

When I tell jokes about the alcoholic, I am
not belittling the person. I am making fun of
the disease that nearly killed me. For me to
live with the disease, I need to be able to laugh
at the disease — in this way I stop it from
having power in my life.

Also I catch something of the symptoms of
the disease in the jokes: the grandiosity,
arrogance, manipulation, insanity, ego, selfishness and exaggeration. The joke allows me to
face reality with a smile.

O God, thank You for the healing gift of humor.

*"The madman who knows that he is mad is close
to sanity."*
                              Juan Ruiz de Alarcon

An alcoholic who continues to drink is
committing suicide. An addict who continues
to use is committing suicide. An overeater who
continues to eat compulsively and destructively
is committing suicide. Madness.

It is like a man standing in the town square
stabbing himself with a knife and asking the
passers-by, "Why am I bleeding?"

Today I accept my past destructive behavior
and try to change it on a daily basis. Spirituality
is loving yourself enough to "see" the writing
on the wall and do something about it. Change
is sanity for the madman!

*God, You seem to have given me a dose of
insanity. Let me use it to Your glory.*

"A society that gives to one class all the opportunities for leisure, and to another class all the burdens of work, dooms both classes to spiritual sterility."
Lewis Mumford

Spirituality brings with it balance. In order to be relaxed, healthy and alive, I need both work and leisure. For me I need to remember it is okay to take a day off; to stay in and relax is not a waste; play time is creative time!

I was not only compulsive around alcohol and people but I was also obsessive about work. I was — and am — a work-aholic. I need to remember to H.A.L.T.: **Don't get too Hungry. Don't get too Angry. Don't get too Lonely. Don't get too Tired.**

Work for me can be a form of escape. In leisure I have the opportunity to meet with myself.

Go on — enjoy yourself, with yourself!

You, who made me a laborer in the vineyard, also expected me to sit and enjoy it.

*"It is not necessary to get away from human
nature but to alter its inner attitude of
heart and mind."*

J. F. Newton

An understanding of sobriety and serenity
that has proved helpful to me is that we are
not only changing but involved in change. We
determine the results of the change.

I can change for good or bad. I can stay sober
or drink. I can be cheerful and creative or
negative and destructive. My attitude deter-
mines the results of my changing life.

Spirituality has been given, but it also needs
to be nurtured. I need to surround myself with
loving and honest people if I am to allow my
spirituality to grow in my life. My continued
willingness is essential to my sobriety and
serenity.

*Thank You for making me with a mind and heart
that together create the action.*

INDEX

373